The Third "How to" Handbook for Jewish Living

The Third "How to" Handbook for Jewish Living

By Rabbi Ron Isaacs
and
Rabbi Kerry Olitzky

KTAV PUBLISHING HOUSE, INC.
HOBOKEN, NEW JERSEY
2002

Library of Congress Cataloging-in-Publication Data

Isaacs, Ronald H.
  The third "how to handbook for Jewish living" / by Ron Isaacs and Kerry Olitzky.
      p. cm.
Includes bibliographical references and index.
  ISBN 0-88125-713-3
  1. Judaism--Customs and practices. 2. Jewish way of life. I. Title:
How to handbook for Jewish living. II. Olitzky, Kerry M. III. Title.
  BM700 .I725 2002
  296.7--dc21

                              2002023827

              Manufactured in the United States of America
   KTAV Publishing House, 900 Jefferson Street, PO Box 6249, Hoboken, NJ 07030
                      Email: info@ktav.com

Table of Contents

For

Mitch Frumkin, President of Congregation B'nai Tikvah,
North Brunswick, NJ

KO

and

Students of the Hebrew High School of
Temple Sholom, Bridgewater, NJ

RI

Introduction

Some will see this book as just another list of "stuff" that has to be done according to a prescribed order for it to be considered "authentic" or literate Judaism. And because the task of doing it all seems overwhelming, they may have trouble finding an organizing principle behind it all. As a result, they will flip through the book, then maybe place it on the shelf, planning to look at it more thoroughly when the need arises. Admittedly, Jewish practice is somewhat forbidding for many people.

Others will want everything carefully plotted out, from the outset, of even the table of contents. So they may turn away from this volume and look for what may appear as a more orderly presentation (although one can consult the index in the back of this volume for an alphabetical listing). Still others will see this volume as a continuation of the clearly presented, step-by-step method of the two "How to" handbooks that preceded it. These readers will understand that one does not have to enter Jewish life in an orderly way, starting with the first of the Jewish year or a particular age. Instead, it is better to just jump in—and then look for help along the way as one encounters the challenges of everyday living. That is what this book (and its authors) are here to do: offer help along the way.

As we live Jewish lives, we are guided by a certain rhythm. Daily prayers, weekly Torah readings, holidays and special occasions. Most of these have been treated in previous volumes. However, as we go about our daily lives, we encounter challenges that are not so orderly or rhythmic or anticipated, and we want to help our readers—and our students—with these challenges, as well. Hence, volume three of the *"How to" Handbook for Jewish Living* series.

Rabbi Ron ("Reeve") Isaacs
Rabbi Kerry ("Shia") Olitzky
Purim 5762

Acknowledgments

We want to thank the many people who responded so enthusiastically to volumes one and two of this series, making many suggestions along the way. Many people requested more details, more "how-to" help. Some of these requests are incorporated in this third volume. We also want to thank the many students—children and adults—who allowed us to work with them to make sure that this step-by-step method actually works. In particular, we thank the members of Temple Sholom in Bridgewater, New Jersey and the many people whose Jewish lives are enhanced by the Jewish Outreach Institute in New York City.

Appreciation is extended to Bernard and Sol Scharfstein of KTAV for supporting us in this project and many others. Their friendship and nurturing extends far beyond the boundaries of a publisher-author relationship. And we are indebted to them, as is the entire Jewish community.

We extend our heartfelt thanks to the members of our families, for their support and their love. Moreover, we thank our children for helping us to remember the steps in basic skill learning as they continue to navigate their lives as emerging adults in the Jewish community.

We also thank the following:

The Rabbinical Assembly for permission to quote from: *The Rabbinical Assembly Rabbi's Manual Volume I,* edited by Rabbi Perry Raphael Rank and Rabbi Gordon M. Freeman © 1998 by the Rabbinical Assembly.

Rabbi Daniel B. Syme for permission to quote from "Talking About God" which appeared in the August/September 1986 issue of *Hadassah Magazine.*

Rabbi Susan Grossman for permission to use her translation of Woman of Valor.

Excerpt from *Healing of Soul, Healing of Body* © 1994 Edited by Simkha Weintraub (Woodstock, VT: Jewish Lights Publishing). $14.95 + $3.50 s/h. Order by mail or call 800-962-4544 or on-line at www.jewishlights.com. Permission granted by Jewish Lights Publishing, P.O. Box 237, Woodstock, VT 05091.

Interpret Dreams

The source:

Babylonian Talmud, *Berakhot* 56b–57b.

What you need to know:

1. Almost all people dream. Dreams are a necessary outlet for the mind.

2. Professional dream interpreters were prominent in ancient Mesopotamia and Egypt, and manuals since that time have revealed hundreds of dream interpretations.

3. Dream interpretation has been a major component of psychoanalysis since that discipline was born. Freud and his disciples spent a great deal of time applying their knowledge to the field of dream study.

4. While many believe that the importance of dreams was neglected until the advent of psychology, Jewish sources spoke of the meaning of dreams centuries ago. The Torah itself, in the stories of Joseph and Pharaoh, emphasizes that dreams are a matter to be dealt with seriously.

5. The Bible often views dreams as signs or omens. The book of Daniel is filled with them. Daniel gains his reputation as an interpreter of dreams for Nebuchadnezzar, the king of Babylon (Daniel 2). He interprets a second dream for the king (Daniel 3:31–5:30) and then wrestles with the meaning of his own dream (Daniel 7). Many Talmudic sages discussed dreams and taught specific doctrines about them. A variety of symbols that may present themselves in dreams are also discussed in rabbinic literature. Here are some basic teachings (taken from the Babylonian Talmud, *Berakhot* 56b–57b):

   i. If you see a reed in a dream, you may hope for wisdom.
   ii. If you dream of an ox that eats flesh, you will become rich.

1

iii. If you dream of riding on an ox, you will rise to greatness.

iv. If you see a donkey in a dream, you may hope for salvation.

v. If you see white grapes in a dream, that is a good sign.

vi. If you see an elephant in a dream, a miracle will occur.

vii. If you see wheat in a dream, you will see peace.

viii. If you see myrtle in your dream, you will have good luck with your property.

ix. If you see a goose in a dream, then you may hope for wisdom.

x. If you dream that you are entering a large town, your desire will be fulfilled.

xi. If you dream that you are sitting in a small boat, you will acquire a good name.

xii. If you dream that you go up on a roof, you will attain a high position.

Things to remember

"Neither a good dream nor a bad dream is wholly fulfilled" (Babylonian Talmud, *Berakhot* 55a).

Key words and phrases:

Chalom: Dream

If you want to know more:

Solomon ben Almoli, *Dream Interpretations from Classical Jewish Sources*. Translated and annotated by Yaakov Elman. Hoboken, NJ: KTAV Publishing House, 1996.

Ronald Isaacs, *Divination, Magic and Healing: The Book of Jewish Folklore*. Northvale, NJ: Jason Aronson, 1998.

Ameliorate a Bad Dream

The source:

Babylonian Talmud, *Ta'anit* 12b; *Berakhot* 55b.

What you need to know:

1. Many famous Talmudic teachers frequently discussed dreams and developed their own interpretations of them, as well as ways to deal with them.

2. Some of these teachers believed that a person's dreams were a direct result of his or her thoughts from the day that immediately preceded it.

3. Fasting became customary in rabbinic times when a person had a bad dream. (In Hebrew, this fast was called a *ta'anit chalom*.)

4. Giving *tzedakah* may also help, say the Sages.

5. The rabbinic sages suggested some verses to be recited upon awakening from a bad dream. For instance, when Samuel the sage had a bad dream, he used to say: "The dreams speak falsely" (Zechariah 10:2). They also instituted a special prayer that was supposed to nullify a dream. This was called *hatavat chalom*. In some synagogues, the nullification prayer is said by congregants as they are being blessed by the descendants of the priests (in *Birkat HaKohanim* during the *Amidah*). This time was chosen in the liturgy because this portion of prayer is a time of general good will. This is the nullification prayer text:

If one has seen a dream and does not remember what one saw, let that person stand before the priests at the time when they spread out their hands and say as follows: "Sovereign of the Universe, I am Yours and my dreams are Yours. I have dreamt a dream and I do not know what it is. Whether I have dreamt about myself or my companions have dreamt about me, or I have dreamt about others, if they are good dreams, confirm them and reinforce them like the dreams of Joseph. If they require a remedy, heal them, as the waters of Marah were healed by Moses, our teacher, and as Miriam was healed of her leprosy, and Hezekiah of his sickness, and the waters of Jericho by Elisha. As you did turn the curse of the wicked Bilaam into a blessing, so turn all my dreams into something good for me."

One should conclude one's nullification prayer at the same time as the priests conclude their benediction, so that surrounding worshipers may answer "Amen" (may it be so). If one is unable to conclude the prayer at the same time as the priests, then, according to the Talmud, one should conclude by saying: "You who are majestic on high, who abides in might, You who are peace and Your name is peace, may it be Your will to bestow peace upon us" (Babylonian Talmud, *Berakhot* 55b)

5. The Talmud also prescribes a procedure for turning an evil dream into a good one. This procedure takes its lead from the number three. Three verses are recited, three instances of the dream are good, and so on. This procedure is suggested in the Talmud as follows:

Rabbi Huna ben Ammi said in the name of Rabbi Pedat, who heard it from Rabbi Yochanan: If a person has a dream which makes one sad, one should go and have it interpreted in the presence of three. Has not Rabbi Chisda said: A dream which is not interpreted is like a letter which is not read and therefore can do no harm? Say, rather, then, one should have a good construction given to it in the presence of three. Let one bring three and say to them: I have seen a good dream. And they will say to that one: Good it is and good may it be. May the All-Merciful turn it to good. Seven times may it be decreed from heaven that it should be good and may it be good. They should say three verses with the word *hafakh* (turn) and three with the word *padach* (redeem) and three with the word *shalom* (peace):

These three verses with the word "turn":

1. "You did **turn** for me my mourning into dancing. You did loosen my sackcloth and gird me with gladness" (Psalm 30:12).

2. "Then shall the virgin rejoice in the dance, and the young men and the old together. For I will **turn** mourn-

4

ing into joy and will comfort them and make them rejoice from their sorrow" (Jeremiah 31:13).

3. "Nevertheless, Adonai your God would not hearken unto Bilaam, but the Lord your God **turned** the curse into a blessing for you" (Deuteronomy 23:6).

These three verses with the word "redeem":

1. "God has **redeemed** my soul in peace, so that none can come near to me" (Psalm 55:19).

2. "And the **redeemed** of Adonai shall return and come with singing to Zion, and sorrow and sighing shall flee away" (Isaiah 35:10).

3. "The people said to Saul: Shall Jonathan die, who has wrought this great salvation in Israel? . . . So the people **redeemed** Jonathan that he died not" (I Samuel 14:45).

These three verses with the word "peace":

1. "'**Peace**, peace to the one who is far and to the one who is near,' says God, who creates the fruits of the lips; and I will heal that person" (Isaiah 57:19).

2. "Then the spirit clothed Amasai, who was chief of the captains: Yours are we, David, and on your side, you, son of Yishai: **Peace**, peace be unto you and peace be your helpers, for your God helps you" (I Chronicles, 12:19).

3. "Thus you shall say: All hail, and **peace** be both to you and peace be to your house, and peace be to all that you have" (I Samuel 25:6).

Things to remember:

The Talmudic sages were known to provide a variety of instructions concerning what to do after dreaming a particular kind of dream. The Talmud also presents a long list of symbols that might be found in a dream and the things that these symbols represent. Most of these are found in the Babylonian Talmud, *Berakhot* 56b–57b. For further details, see the section entitled "Interpreting Dreams" in this "How to" handbook.

Key words and phrases:

Chalom: Dream
Hatavat Chalom: Prayer for nullifying a dream
Ta'anit Chalom: Dream fast

If you want to know more:

Solomon ben Almoli, *Dream Interpretations from Classical Jewish Sources*. Translated and annotated by Yaakov Elman. Hoboken, NJ: KTAV Publishing Co., 1996.
Shmuel Boteach, *Dreams*. Brooklyn: B.P., 1991.

Add Meaning to the Bar/Bat Mitzvah Party

The source:

There is no classic source for this "How to".

What you need to know:

1. The festive meal that follows the ceremony of bar or bat mitzvah is an opportunity for family and friends to celebrate the joy (*simcha*) of the occasion. The meal after the religious ceremony is called a *seudat mitzvah* (religious meal). It may take some effort to create a context in which the party takes on an aura of sanctity.

2. Since many families have already developed ways that invest the party with added sanctity, here are some simple ideas that work:

   i. Instead of using flowers as centerpieces, use Jewish books as your table decorations. Then donate the books to your local synagogue library or community center.

   ii. With each place card, include information about MAZON: A Jewish Response to Hunger. Encourage your guests to contribute to it.

   iii. In advance, arrange to give leftover food to a local food bank.

   iv. Instead of giving souvenir party favors to the guests, plant trees in Israel in their honor and give out the tree certificates as mementoes.

   v. Ask guests to bring canned food, clothing, or toys to the party for distribution to the needy.

   vi. Give a percentage of the total cost of your Bar/Bat Mitzvah celebration to a hunger relief organization.

   vii. Be sure to begin your meal with the *hamotzi*, the blessing over the bread.

   viii. Be sure to conclude your meal with the *birkat hamazon*, the blessing after the meal. The text for both *hamotzi* and *birkat hamazon* can be printed in booklets with explanations and guidelines so that people can continue to adopt the practices as part of their home routine.

ix. Instead of a D.J. or band, consider Israeli dancing and Jewish music to help further invest the party with deeper Jewish feeling. As an alternative, use these when the band or D.J. takes a break.

Things to remember:

In 1595 in Cracow, Poland, the rabbinic authorities levied a communal tax on bar mitzvah feasts so as to keep them within the bounds of good taste. Judaism has always urged people to use moderation in their celebrations to ensure that the spiritual significance of the event is not lost.

Key words and phrases:

Birkat Hamazon: Blessing after the meal
Hamotzi: Blessing over the bread
Seudat Mitzvah: Religious meal

If you want to know more:

Ronald H. Isaacs, *Reaching for Sinai: A Practical Handbook for Bar/Bat Mitzvah and Family*. Hoboken, NJ: KTAV Publishing House, Inc., 1999.
Jeffrey K. Salkin, *Putting God on the Guest List*. Woodstock, VT: Jewish Lights Publishing, 1992.

Prepare a Meaningful Passover Family *Seder*

The source:

Mishnah, *Pesachim* 10.

What you need to know:

1. It is a tradition on the first two nights of Passover to have a family gathering and recite the narrative of Passover using the *Haggadah*. This gathering is known as the Passover *seder*. As a result, more Jews celebrate the Passover *seder* in one form or another than any other holiday observance, including Hanukkah.

2. Make the *seder* interactive. Even if the gathering is all adult, use props, games, and engaging questions. Keep the *seder* lively.

3. Here are some suggestions to help lift up the *seder*.

   i. **Karpas**: Although it is early evening, go outside. Find a new spring blossom and recite the special blessing when you see a blossom or flower for the first time: "Praised are You, Adonai, Sovereign of the universe, who has not left the world lacking in anything and has created in it good trees to give pleasure to people." While this blessing can be recited at various times of the year (during the spring or late winter), it is only recited once a year according to tradition.

   ii. **Yachatz**: Place the afikoman in a bag and throw it over your shoulder. Have participants rise and follow the leader as he or she carries the afikoman around the *seder* table in a reenactment of the Exodus.

   iii. **Ma Nishtana**: Ask additional contemporary questions during the Ma Nishtana part of the *seder*. For example, "Why must the proliferation of nuclear weapons continue?" or "Why is there homelessness when our society is so wealthy?"

iv. **Maggid**: An interesting custom is to have the leader or one of the participants leave the room and return with a napkin containing the afikoman slung over one's shoulder. Everyone at the table then asks: "Who are you?" The answer from the person acting out the Exodus: "A Jew." The dialogue continues: "Where do you come from?" "From Egypt." "What did you do there?" "I was a slave." How many years did it take for you to come here?" "Forty years." Let the dialogue continue.

v. **Ten Plagues**: Ask the participants to list ten contemporary plagues which "plague" us today. In addition, prepare simulations for each of the ten plagues in advance. For example: for blood, use magic trick blood that changes water to blood; for frogs, use rubber frogs; for lice, use plastic bugs. You get the idea. As the plagues are read, have *seder* participants open the bags and show the "plague."

vi. **Afikoman**: Play the Afikoman game. Participants sing a Passover song while the "searcher" looks for the afikoman. As the searcher gets closer to the afikoman, those at the Seder table sing the song more loudly. As the searcher moves further away from the afikoman, the participants sing more softly.

vii. **Elijah the Prophet**: Have a participant leave in advance and re-enter, dressed as Elijah. Then give participants a chance to ask Elijah questions about himself, his life and the purpose of his visit.

viii. **Sing Chad Gadya:** Take each character in the story in Chad Gadya and as you sing the song and the character or object is about to be sung, create a sound for the character. For example, when the cat is mentioned, someone says "meow." When the dog is mentioned someone says "bow wow." It may sound childish, but take it from us, it is a lot of fun with families and friends.

Things to remember:

The *Haggadah* is not just a book of stories from the distant past. It is a living record of Jewish history which we add to each year as we participate in the *seder*. Thus, we are reminded during the *seder* that we must feel as if we were in Egypt ourselves and were personally freed. Invite participants to talk about what it was like when they were slaves in Egypt. Have them also share one of the first things that they would have done once they were liberated.

Key words and phrases:

Haggadah: Book read at the *seder* that contains the narrative of the Israelite journey from slavery into freedom

Seder: Passover meal

If you want to know more:

Philip Goodman, *The Passover Anthology*. Philadelphia: Jewish Publication Society, 1961.

Ronald Isaacs, *Every Person's Guide to Passover*. Northvale, NJ: Jason Aronson, 1999.

Ben Kamin, *Think Passover*. New York: Dutton, 1997.

Joy Leavitt and Michael Strassfeld, *A Night of Questions*. Philadelphia: Reconstructionist Press, 2000.

Rachel Musleah, *Why on This Night: A Passover Haggadah for Family Celebration*. New York: Aladdin Paperbacks/Simon & Schuster, 2000.

Kerry M. Olitzky and Ronald H. Isaacs, *The Discovery Haggadah*. Hoboken, NJ: KTAV Publishing, 1992.

Shoshana Silberman, *In Every Generation: A Family Haggadah*. Rockville, MD: Kar-Ben Copies, 1987.

A Survivor's Haggadah. Philadelphia: Jewish Publication Society, 2000.

Noam Zion and David Dishon, *A Different Night*. Jerusalem: Shalom Hartman Institute, 1997.

Celebrate Lag B'Omer

The source:

Leviticus 23:15–16: "You shall count from the day after [the first day of] Passover, when an *omer* of grain is brought as an offering, seven complete weeks".

What you need to know:

1. Lag B'Omer, literally the "33rd day of the Omer" occurs on the 18th day of Iyar. It serves as a break in the semi-mourning *sefirah* days between Passover and Shavuot.

2. Many synagogues hold picnics and outings on Lag B'Omer, with food, music, dance, sporting events (often in the form of a competitive Maccabiah), and other festivities. Some synagogues hold bonfires and cook-outs on Lag B'Omer, which often include Israeli singing and dancing. If your synagogue does not have a Lag B'Omer program, be the first to start one.

3. Use the occasion to go on a family outing or picnic.

4. Get together with several families and make a campfire which includes good eating and singing.

5. Each night, before the counting of the omer (which begins on the second evening of Passover), take a non-perishable grain product and place it in a box. On Lag B'Omer, take all of the grain products to a local food pantry as your way of helping the hungry.

More particulars

Lag B'Omer is not a major holiday. It is not mentioned in the Bible and there are no specific prayers associated with it. However, there are several historical events that have been associated with the holiday. In Roman times, according to tradition, a great plague which ravaged the students of Rabbi Akiva came to an end on the 18th of Iyar, which is Lag B'Omer. Another tradition concerns Rabbi Shimon bar Yochai, a disciple of Rabbi Akiva, who was sentenced to death by the Romans for his participation in a revolt against them. He hid in a cave and did not come out until Lag B'Omer, when he learned that the enemy had been defeated. Because of the connection to Rabbi Akiva and his students, Lag B'Omer is also known as the Scholar's Festival, and Jewish children throughout the world hold special celebrations to mark the occasion.

Key words and phrases:

Lag: Hebrew letters (*lamed-gimel*) with the alpha-numeric value of 33

Omer: Measure of barley brought to the Temple on the second day of Passover. From that day we count every day until Shavuot to show the connection between the two holidays.

If you want to know more:

Ronald H. Isaacs and Kerry M. Olitzky, *Sacred Celebrations: A Jewish Holiday Handbook*. Hoboken, NJ: KTAV Publishing, 1994.

Kerry M. Olitzky and Rachel Smookler, *Anticipating Revelation: Counting Our Way Through the Desert: An Omer Calendar of the Spirit*. New York: Synagogue 2000, 1998.

Improve your *Derekh Eretz*

The source:

Various sections of *Shabbat, Pesachim, Baba Kamma,* and *Derekh Eretz Zuta* in the Babylonian Talmud; as well as the entire book of Proverbs and the mishnah of *Pirke Avot.*

What you need to know:

1. *Derekh Eretz* is a term referring to good behavior, courtesy, politeness, etiquette.

2. The rabbis were intent on setting rules of behavior to establish a good name for oneself and promote the welfare of society.

3. The Talmudic tractate called *Derekh Eretz Zuta* is a collection of ethical teachings containing rules of conduct. It urges gentleness, patience, respect for age, readiness to forgive. Many of its teachings are directed to scholars.

4. Following are ten guidelines for improving your *derekh eretz* as culled from various rabbinic sources:

    1. **Address people by their names**: "A person spoken to must first be addressed by one's name, just as God first called to Moses and then spoke to him." (Babylonian Talmud, *Yoma* 4b)
    2. **Do not suddenly enter a neighbor's home, but wait until someone opens the door:** "The answer 'yes' to a knock on the door does not mean enter but wait." (Babylonian Talmud, *Baba Kamma* 33a)
    3. **Be careful with your words:** "Rabbi Joshua ben Levi said: Never use an indecent expression, even if you have to use more words to complete the sentence." (Babylonian Talmud, *Pesachim* 3a)
    4. **Be humble**: "God is a friend of the person who is humble." (Zohar ii, 233b)
    5. **Be compassionate:** "The person who has compassion for other people will receive compassion from Heaven." (Babylonian Talmud, *Shabbat* 151b)
    6. **After offending, be sure to reconcile:** "Whoever

offends one's fellow human being, even if only with words, should endeavor to reconcile with that person." (Babylonian Talmud, *Yoma* 87a)

7. **When criticizing, do so in a *menschlikhkeit* way:** "A person who rebukes another should administer the rebuke privately, speak to the offender gently and tenderly, and point out that he is speaking only for the wrongdoer's own good. (Maimonides, *Mishneh Torah*, Laws Concerning Moral Dispositions and Ethical Conduct 6:7.)

8. **Don't meddle:** "Do not inject yourself into someone else's quarrel. It's none of your business!" (*Sefer Chasidim,* paragraph 73)

9. **Be a happy person:** "A happy heart is good medicine." (Proverbs 17:22)

10. **Be generous:** "One who says: what is mine is yours, and what is yours is yours, is saintly. (*Pirke Avot* 4:12)

11. **Overlook an insult:** A person should overlook an insult and not glorify himself by his fellow person's humiliation. (*Derekh Eretz Zuta* 6:4)

Things to remember:

Pirke Avot 5:19 sums up the ideal character in this way:

Whoever has these three attributes is of the disciples of our ancestor Abraham: a good eye, a humble mind, and a lowly spirit.

Key words and phrases:

Derekh Eretz: Proper behavior

If you want to know more:

Ronald H. Isaacs *The Jewish Book of Etiquette*. Northvale, NJ: Jason Aronson, 1998.

S. Wagschal, *Guide to Derech Eretz*. New York: Feldheim Publishers, 1993.

Kerry M. Olitzky and Rachel T. Sabath, *Striving Toward Virtue: A Contemporary Guide for Jewish Ethical Behavior*. Hoboken: NJ: KTAV Publishing, 1996.

Annul a Vow

The source:

Kitzur Shulchan Arukh, chapter 67 (section on vows and oaths).

Things to remember:

1. Judaism is a religion of values and concepts which is deeply invested in words. The power of words, when spoken in the form of a promise, is likened to a belief in God, in whose name that vow is made.

2. Jewish law requires that one must keep a commitment, for commitments are tied to one's belief in God and in God's presence in the world and in the lives of people.

3. Rabbinic advice generally states that one should avoid making vows.

4. When wanting to annul a vow one should consult one's local rabbi. According to the *Code of Jewish Law,* vows made to consecrate certain objects to God must be fulfilled. ("I will pay my vows to God" Psalm 116:18).

5. Following is a formula for annulling a vow, which is customarily done on the morning before Rosh Hashanah in the presence of three, who constitute an improvised court:

   I request annulment for the vows that I have made, whether they were matters relating to money, or to the body, or whether they were matters related to the soul.

   The three members of the "court" repeat three times: May everything be permitted you, may everything be forgiven you, may everything be allowed you.

   The petitioner concludes: Behold, I make formal declaration before you and I cancel from this time onward all vows and oaths. Regarding all of them, I regret them from this time and forever.

Things to remember:

1. The popular Hebrew expression *blee neder* (without vow), accompanying any statement concerning some future action contemplated by the speaker, is in keeping with the idea that we are expected to carry out everything we say, unless we specify that it is not a solemn promise but a mere thought expressed in words.

2. Before you think otherwise, please note that the annulment of vows does not pertain to vows that were made to other people, especially those involving financial obligations.

More particulars

The best-known statement about promises and vows occurs on the eve of Yom Kippur, the Day of Atonement, at the Kol Nidre Service. This declaration specifies that all the promises that one has made to God that have gone unfulfilled are null and void.

Key words and phrases:

Blee Neder: Without vow
Hatarat nedarim: The annulment of vows
Neder: Vow

If you want to know more:

Solomon Ganzfried, *Code of Jewish Law* (Abridged). New York: Hebrew Publishing Company, 1961.

Choose a Synagogue

The source:

"Let them make Me a sanctuary, so I may dwell among them" (Exodus 25:8).

What you need to know:

1. The Israelites built a tabernacle to God in the wilderness in Bible times. There they offered sacrifices to God.

2. It is likely that the synagogue originated after the destruction of the First Temple when those exiled to Babylonia would gather together for mutual strength and consolation. After the destruction of the Second Temple, the synagogue became the only method of worship.

3. Your local synagogue can be a most powerful ally in realizing the Jewish aspirations you have for yourself and your children.

4. Some synagogues, by virtue of the caliber of their rabbinic and lay leadership, set religious, moral, and ethical expectations for a congregation. Families should seek out a congregation that will help them maintain religious standards with which they are comfortable and grow spiritually.

3. When seeking out a synagogue, call the local Jewish Federation to get the names of ones in your area. You will want to begin by finding out whether there is a local synagogue that matches the branch of Judaism with which you feel most comfortable (e.g., Orthodox, Conservative, Reform, Reconstructionist).

4. Begin by making an appointment with the rabbi to determine the mission statement of the synagogue, the rabbi's philosophy, educational goals of the religious school, and so forth.

5. Meet with the synagogue's educational director to discuss the school's curriculum, its teaching staff, and teaching mission.

6. Ask to see copies of the Adult Education brochure and a brochure that details and describes all of the offerings and organizations within the synagogue (e.g., Sisterhood, Men's Club, Couples Club, and Youth groups).

7. Speak to families that are already members to determine their evaluation of the synagogue and its professional staff.

8. Try to attend a worship service and several programs to get a sense of the culture of the synagogue and its members.

Things to remember:

1. If you are newly married, many synagogues will offer you a free year's membership.

2. Synagogues will be prepared to make a special arrangement if you feel that paying full dues is an undue financial hardship. Also, they often have a special rate for families whose head of household is under 30 years of age.

3. No human institution has a longer continuous history than the synagogue, and none has done more for the uplifting of the human race.

Key words and phrases:

Bet Knesset: Synagogue
Shule: Yiddish for "synagogue"

If you want to know more:

Hayim Halevy Donin, *To Pray as a Jew*. New York: Basic Books, 1980.

Do *Ushpizin* for Sukkot

The source:

Zohar 5:103b.

What you need to know:

1. According to the tradition of kabbalah, these seven mystical guests visit the sukkah during the days of the festival of Sukkot: Abraham, Isaac, Jacob, Moses, Aaron, Joseph and David

2. Recently, some people have advocated inviting the matriarchs and other important women of the Bible and in Jewish life to also be *ushpizin* guests in the sukkah. The most popular list includes: Sarah, Rebecca, Rachel, Leah, Miriam, Abigail and Esther.

3. Invite the spiritual guest of each day before the meal, using this text as invitation: "Enter, exalted guests. Be seated, guests of faithfulness. Be seated in the shade of the Holy Blessed One. Worthy is our portion, worthy is the portion of Israel, as it is written: 'For God's portion is God's people, Jacob the lot of God's heritage.' For the sake of the unification of the Holy Blessed One and God's Presence, to unify the Name *Yud-Hei* with *Vav-Hei* in perfect unity through God who is hidden and inscrutable. May the pleasantness of my God be upon us. May God establish our handiwork for us."

4. Sephardic Jews set aside an ornate chair for the honored guest and recite: "This is the chair of the *ushpizin*."

5. Rabbi Zalman Schachter-Shalomi suggests that one treat each *ushpizin* as a real presence in the sukkah. Set aside a chair for him or her. Try to see the world through the eyes of an Abraham or Rachel. What idols would Abraham smash today? If you are with your family or some other group, ask each person to have a conversation with the *ushpizin*.

Things to remember:

1. Decorate the sukkah with a wall plaque which bears an inscription of the seven guests.

2. Some families have the custom of making up a list of their contemporary heroes, and each night having a different family member invite a new imaginary guest into the sukkah. This activity can be enhanced by having a family member "role play" a contemporary guest. Family members are asked to guess the identity of the contemporary guest.

More particulars

There is an interesting connection between the *ushpizin* and Sukkot. All of the *ushpizin* were wanderers or exiles. Abraham left his father's house to go to Israel. All three patriarchs wandered in the land of Canaan, dealing with the rulers from a position of disadvantage. Jacob fled to Laban. Joseph was exiled from his family. Moses fled Egypt for Midian. Together with Aaron, Moses led the people for forty years as they wandered in the desert. David fled from Saul. The theme of wandering and homelessness symbolized by the temporariness of the sukkah is reflected in the lives of the *ushpizin*.

Key words and phrases:

Ushpizin: Guests

If you want to know more:

Ronald Isaacs and Kerry M. Olitzky, *Sacred Celebrations: A Jewish Holiday Handbook*. Hoboken: NJ: KTAV Publishing, 1994.

Spiritualize Your Morning Waking Moments

The source

Code of Jewish Law (Abridged) Chapter 1: Rules of Conduct upon Arising in the Morning.

What you need to know:

1. According to Jewish tradition, an individual is encouraged to direct one's mind to God and to be aware of God's presence, as soon as he or she awakens in the morning.

2. The first traditional practice upon awakening is the recitation of the prayer for thankfulness to God, named by its opening words, *Modeh Ani* (I thank You). The text of this prayer can be found at the beginning of most prayer books. It is a response to the statement from the previous evening before sleep. At that time one gives one's soul into God's hands for safekeeping. At that time one says: "Into Your hand I commit my spirit." In the morning one expresses gratitude at receiving it back:

מוֹדֶה* אֲנִי לְפָנֶיךָ, מֶלֶךְ חַי וְקַיָּם, שֶׁהֶחֱזַרְתָּ בִּי נִשְׁמָתִי בְּחֶמְלָה רַבָּה אֱמוּנָתֶךָ.

*females say: מוֹדָה

Modeh ani lefanekha melekh chai v'kayam she-he-che-zarta bee nishmatee be'chemlah; rabbah emunatekha.

I am grateful to You, living and enduring Sovereign, for restoring my soul to me in compassion. You are faithful beyond measure.

3. The second practice required by traditional Jewish law is the ritual of washing of the hands. Jewish mystics explains this practice: When we sleep, the holy soul departs, and an unclean spirit rests in our body. When we awaken, this unclean spirit departs from

the entire body except the fingers, from which it does not pass until water is poured on them with this blessing:

בָּרוּךְ אַתָּה יְיָ אֱלֹהֵינוּ מֶלֶךְ הָעוֹלָם אֲשֶׁר קִדְּשָׁנוּ בְּמִצְוֹתָיו, וְצִוָּנוּ עַל נְטִילַת יָדָיִם:

Barukh ata Adonai Eloheinu melekh ha'olam asher kidshanu be'mitzvotav v'tzivanu al nitalat yadayim.

Praised are You, Adonai our God, Sovereign of the Universe, who adds holiness to our life and who has given us the *mitzvah* of washing our hands.

4. After handwashing it is a good idea to direct your mind to God and God's service through meditation, and to remind yourself of reverence for God. An excellent *kavanna* (sacred mantra) for this purpose is also found in the early pages of most prayer books:

אֱלֹהַי! נְשָׁמָה שֶׁנָּתַתָּ בִּי טְהוֹרָה הִיא.

Elohai neshama sh'nata bee tehorah hee
God, the soul that you have given me is pure.

Key words and phrases:

Modeh Ani: Thank you
Netilat yadayim: Washing the hands

If you want to know more:

Yitzhak Buxbaum, *Jewish Spiritual Practices*. Northvale, NJ: Jason Aronson, 1990.
Solomon Ganzfried, *Code of Jewish Law* (Abridged). New York: Hebrew Publishing Company, 1961.

The source:

1. "You shall not cook a kid in its mother's milk." (Exodus 23:19)

2. "You shall set apart the ritually clean beast from the unclean." (Leviticus 20:25)

3. "You must not eat flesh torn by beasts." (Exodus 22:30)

4. "You shall not eat anything that died a natural death." (Deuteronomy 14:21)

What you need to know:

1. *Kashrut* is about holiness and spiritual direction. It is not about health and hygiene (although both may be a benefit of keeping kosher).

2. The laws of *kashrut* regulate eating. Jews are not permitted to eat whatever they may want. Even permitted foods must be prepared in a special way. For instance, the only animals designated by the Torah as kosher are those that have cloven hooves and that chew their cud (i.e., process their food through regurgitation). But even these animals must be slaughtered by a *shochet* (ritual slaughterer).

3. Among fish, only those with fins and scales are designated kosher.

4. Jewish law forbids consuming an animal's blood. It was not enough that the animal must be killed in the most humane way, but even the symbol of life, the blood, must be removed.

5. In three separate places in the Torah, the Torah legislates that one shall not seethe a kid in its mother's milk. The rabbis deduced from this that not only is it forbidden to cook meat and milk products together but also to eat them or derive any benefit from them. The rabbis also forbade the eating of meat and milk together at the same meal even if they were not cooked together. Be-

cause of this law, kosher homes have two sets of dishes and cutlery, one for meat and the other for dairy.

6. Foods such as fish, fruits, and vegetables, which are neither milk nor meat, are called *pareve* and may be eaten with either milk or meat meals.

7. It is important to remember that within the Jewish community one finds many variations in the way Jews observe the dietary laws. Different authorities prescribe a variety of interpretations.

8. Following are some guidelines for making a home kosher:

   i. The basic requirements for having a kosher kitchen are twofold: there should be nothing nonkosher in it, and it should provide for separation of meat and dairy foods and utensils. Today kosher symbols abound on food products, certifying them as kosher.

   ii. There are two basic methods of *kashering* utensils. Most cooking utensils can be made kosher by immersion in boiling water. This includes metal pots, most pans including nonstick pans, flatware, plastic with high heat tolerance and many other kinds of kitchenware. The procedure is as follows:

      a. Thoroughly scour the article to be made kosher.
      b. Set the article aside and do not use it for 24 hours.
      c. Completely immerse the article in a pot of boiling water.
      d. If the pot is too large to fit into another pot, the pot to be kashered is filled to the brim with water, and that water is brought to a boil. While the water is still boiling, a hot stone or piece of metal is dropped into the pot in order that the water remain at its peak heat and also that it boil over the side of the pot.
      e. Rinse the articles immediately under cold water.
      f. The pot in which the articles were *kashered* is then itself *kashered*.

iii. Any utensil which comes in direct contact with fire, such as a barbecue spit or grill, a broiling pan, or rack, is *kashered* by open flame. The procedure is as follows:

    a. Thoroughly scour the article.

    b. Set the article aside and do not use it for 24 hours.

    c. Put the article under or over an open flame and thoroughly heat it until the metal glows red hot or is so hot that a piece of paper is singed when it is touched to the metal.

iv. Among Conservative Jews, glassware, when washed, is considered as new. However, there is a more elaborate process for *kashering* glassware among Orthodox Jews.

v. A sink is *kashered* like a large pot, by scouring, filling with boiling water, and dropping a hot stone or hot piece of metal into it.

vi. To *kasher* a dishwasher, scour the interior. The dishwasher should then not be used for 24 hours and then it should be run through a complete wash cycle without soap.

vii. To *kasher* a refrigerator/freezer, remove the shelves and bins in order to facilitate cleaning. Then carefully wash the shelves, bins and walls.

viii. Countertops and tables made of formica should be thoroughly scoured. Those made of wood are scraped with a steel brush, and the surface is then left bare for 24 hours. After that the surface is completely splashed with boiling water, poured directly from the pot in which the water was boiled.

ix. To kasher a microwave oven, clean it thoroughly, and place a cup of water inside. The microwave should then be turned on until the water boils out. (But be careful not to let the microwave run too long; you will burn *it* out.)

Key words and phrases:

Fleishig (Yiddish): A product deriving from meat
Kosher: Fit and proper to eat

Kashering: The process of making utensils kosher for use
Kashrut: The system of the Jewish dietary laws
Milchig: A dairy-based food
Pareve: Something neutral, neither meat nor dairy (all eggs, fish, fruits, vegetables and grains are *pareve*)

If you want to know more:

Samuel H. Dresner and Seymour Siegel, *The Jewish Dietary Laws*. New York: Rabbinical Assembly, 1982.

James M. Lebeau, *The Jewish Dietary Laws: Sanctify Life*. New York: United Synagogue Department of Youth Activities, 1983.

Behave in a Synagogue

The source:

Code of Jewish Law (abridged), The Sanctity of Synagogue and the House of Study, Vol. 1, Ch. 13.

What you need to know:

1. Each synagogue has its own *minhag hamakom* (community custom) with regard to behavior and dress, particularly for worship services. Some are Friday night casual and Saturday morning formal—with no special expectations for weekday and Sunday morning *minyanim* (usually dependent on what else is going on or where the worshiper is going following the service). And while certain holidays may be formal (such as Sukkot, Pesach and Shavuot), others may be more casual (such as Hanukkah and Purim). Therefore, it is important to check with the specific synagogue prior to services.

2. There are specific times during which synagogues close the entry doors to the sanctuary, indicating that it is probably an inappropriate time to enter. These usually include the rabbi's sermon (simply a matter of respect) and while the congregation is standing (for example, for the reader's repetition of the *Amidah*).

3. While it may be impolite to speak while others are praying throughout the service (or even when the rabbi is talking), and therefore it is discouraged, there are times in the service when we are actually prohibited by Jewish law from talking. The primary time when we are prohibited from speaking is during the reading of the Torah since, traditionally, we are simulating revelation and listening for God's voice speaking to us (which is rather difficult to do when people are talking). This is the general rule: don't talk while others are praying.

4. Don't wait for "stage directions" from the rabbi. Stand or sit when appropriate. Many prayer books help you

with this if you are unfamiliar with the service. However, the Reform and Conservative movements may differ somewhat as to standing/sitting during certain parts of the service and even congregations within the same movement differ on other parts. If you are unfamiliar with the custom of the congregation, take your cue from someone sitting nearby.

5. In Orthodox, Conservative, and many Reform and Reconstructionist congregations, certain activities are prohibited on Shabbat and holidays, such as using telephones (including cellular telephones) or any other electronic devices, smoking (some synagogues are smoke-free all the time as a health precaution), and the use of cameras. Since it is traditionally forbidden to drive on the Sabbath and holidays, many Orthodox congregations actually secure their parking lots with a chain or gate.

Things to remember:

1. Men can't go wrong dressed in suits. And women can't go wrong in dresses. It is always better to be more formally dressed, rather than more casually dressed. Women should keep their shoulders covered. No sleeveless tops, plunging necklines, or short skirts. Modesty is the goal.

2. Men should keep their head covered. Bring a *kipah* with you (if you do not wear one regularly). While it is customary for women in some synagogues to cover their heads, others only do so if they are married. Even in synagogues where only married women cover their heads, single women may be required to cover their heads when they ascend the *bimah* for an *aliyah* to the Torah. Of course, generally, this is only relevant in an egalitarian congregation.

3. On mornings men should bring a *tallit* with them. However, most synagogues that require men to wear *tallitot* usually have an ample supply available. Yet, when there are many guests (such as during a *bar/bat mitzvah*), this supply dwindles rather rapidly. It is the custom in some congregations for only married men to wear *tallitot*.

However, this presupposes that those unmarried men are each wearing a *tallit katan* under their garments.

4. On mornings during which *tefillin* is worn, men (and women who do so) should bring their *tefillin* with them. Few congregations have an adequate supply for those who do not bring them. And if you need help with putting on *tefillin*, don't be afraid to ask.

Key words and phrases:

Minhag hamakom: prevailing custom of the community or of the synagogue
Tzniut: modesty
Zenut: promiscuous sexual behavior, exploiting the body (the opposite of *tzniut*)

If you want to know more:

Kerry M. Olitzky and Rachel T. Sabath, *Striving Toward Virtue: A Contemporary Guide for Jewish Ethical Behavior*. Hoboken, NJ: KTAV Publishing House, 1996. (See "Exploiting the Body/Protecting the Spirit, pp. 60–67).

More particulars:

Some congregations are used to people coming and going throughout the service. It is ok, goes the logic, to be fashionably late. Others put it rather sharply, "The Reform movement has no *musaf* and the Conservative movement has no *shacharit*." Be on time. Stay for the entire service.

Count a Minyan

The source:

Numbers 14:27, the story of the ten spies; alternatively, Genesis 18:32, where Abraham argues with God on behalf of the possibility of finding ten righteous men in Sodom.

What you need to know:

1. A *minyan* (ten men in Orthodox Judaism or ten men and/or women in other movements) is the minimum number of persons that constitute a religious community; a prayer quorum.

2. A person may hallow God's name by moral acts in private, God's name cannot be hallowed in public prayer unless it is in the presence of a congregation of ten adult "witnesses."

Things to remember:

1. A *minyan* is required for the repetition of the *amidah* with the *kedusha*; reading the Torah and haftarah; reciting the priestly benediction; and the *kaddish*. Most also require a *minyan* for the call to prayer, the invitation of *barekhu*.

2. A *minyan* is required for a mourner to be able to say *kaddish* and thereby be comforted by this "community."

3. A *minyan* is required for the recital of the seven wedding blessings.

4. The Reform movement historically rejected the requirement of *minyan*, although many Reform rabbis have reinstated it.

5. Some Conservative congregations do not count women to make up the requirement of ten adults, but the Reform and Reconstructionist movements do so.

Key words and phrases:

Minyan: literally means number; refers to the smallest unit
of a community

If you want to know more:

Simon Glustrom, *Language of Judaism*. Northvale, NJ: Jason Aronson, 1988.

More particulars:

1. Children are not counted as part of the *minyan*, but a ten-year-old child or older may count as the tenth in the presence of nine adults.

2. A long-standing custom is not to count Jews in order to determine whether a *minyan* is present. Counting in the Bible was often connected to census-taking for wars of aggression. Thus, counting is considered an act that is alien to Judaism. In order to determine if the proper number of people are present for a *minyan*, several ten-word liturgical passages are recommended. For example, *"Hoshiyah et amekha u'varekh et nachalatekha ooreym v'naseym ad olam."* Alternatively, some people add the word "not" (or *nisht* in Yiddish) before each number.

Devise a Mitzvah Performance Plan

The source:

Six hundred and thirteen commandments were commanded to Moses (Babylonian Talmud, *Makkot* 23b).

What you need to know:

1. Set a goal for yourself that you think is feasible. A new mitzvah a day, a week, a month. Work it into your daily routine. Find a place where it is comfortable for you. After it is part of you (and only you know it when you miss it and you *really* miss it), then go on to the next one on your list.

2. While it is easier for members of a family to support one another in the acquisition of *mitzvot*, this is not always possible. So if you can't get family members to join you, then at least ask for their support and understanding.

3. It usually helps to focus on an area or two of *mitzvot*. For example, begin by working on Shabbat *mitzvot* or the *mitzvot* regarding *kashrut* and eating. Then you can easily make the connection from one behavior to another. Sometimes, there are clusters of *mitzvot* that are difficult to separate one from another.

4. Don't focus on what you have ahead of you to do. Instead, concentrate on the progress you have made and luxuriate in each *mitzvah* as it takes you closer in your relationship to God.

5. Make a chart and keep a journal. The goal is not quantity. It is the soulful depth of the experience.

Things to remember:

1. Some people may try to tell you that it is all or nothing. Don't believe them. We grow in *mitzvot* just as we grow in other aspects of our lives. Our relationship with the tradition is dynamic—as it should be.

2. There are several different listings of the 613 commandments.

3. Many of the commandments are restricted to the land of Israel, and the sacrificial system. Therefore, we are unable to fulfill many of them.

4. Often, we learn Jewish behaviors by observing, then emulating (really mimicking) others. Make sure that the person you are following has it right. It is best to develop a relationship with a teacher (like your rabbi) and follow his or her guidance and advice. And don't be afraid to ask questions or ask for assistance.

Key words and phrases:

M'tzaveh: *the* commander, that is, God

Mitzvah: commandment, sacred obligation, a Divine instruction; not to be confused with *mitzveh* (as influenced by the Yiddish) a good deed

Taryag hamitzvot: an abbreviation/acronym for 613 commandments based on the Hebrew alpha-numeric for the number 613

If you want to know more:

Aaron HaLevi, *The Book of Mitzvah Education*, 5 vols. Jerusalem: 1978.

Ronald Isaacs, *The Book of Commandments*. Northvale, NJ: Jason Aronson, 1992.

More particulars:

Most *mitzvot* begin with a blessing. The traditional form of blessing is "*Barukh ata Adonai Elohenu Melekh Ha-olam . . .*" then it continues either with a reference first to *mitzvot* (*asher kidshanu b'mitzvotav v'tzivanu*—who has made us holy with *mitzvot*) or directly to the theme or behavior. This is what Jewish tradition considers the best way to access God's address, so to speak. It is the traditional vehicle for establishing a line of communication, a dialogue with the Divine. Most behaviors are preceded by a blessing. Some, like the ritual washing of hands before eating bread, are done before saying the blessing. Others seem to be delayed, such as the blessing over wine during *Havdalah,* but what is really taking place is the reciting of a series of blessings before drinking the wine.

Do Jewish Meditation

The source:

God can be found wherever God is sought.

What you need to know:

1. Rabbi Zalman Schacter-Shalomi suggests that having a visual image of *kavannah* is important as you try to align your will with the will of God. Thus, close your eyes and visualize God's will flowing through your body, becoming united with your soul and all aspects of your body, flowing through your veins and arteries, filling your limbs, organs, senses, brain, and nerves.

   Some people use the following (from a midrash) as a visualization before meditating:

   > In the name of Adonai, the God of Israel,
   > At my right is Michael (love),
   > at my left is Gabriel (strength),
   > ahead of me is Oriel (light of the mind),
   > behind me is Raphael (healing).
   > Above me—and all around me—is the *Shekhinah* of God.

2. Start out slowly. Perhaps begin with ten minutes the first day. You can start by meditating without a text. Just meditate on God. For help, think about a text that describes something about God, such as "How great are Your works, God" (*Mah rabu maasekha Yah!*). Or choose a text that you are familiar with that brings spiritual pleasure to you. Then repeat it over and over, softly aloud at first, and then just in your head, until the words are indistinguishable one from the other.

2. You may want to meditate only a couple times a week until it has become part of your daily routine and don't rush ahead to find another phrase on which to meditate. The phrase only gets you started until you can transcend it fully. One can meditate for an entire life on just one meditation.

Things to remember:

1. Meditation takes time over time. So plan on spending at least a half hour a day meditating.

2. Meditation is about the direction and intention, the *kavannah*, of your activity. In this case, it is to direct yourself toward God.

3. You can use meditation as part of your prayer and ritual life, as well. Spend a few minutes meditating after you have said a blessing over bread before you eat it, for example. Or use the time to put on *tallit* and *tefillin* in the morning to meditate before reciting the morning service.

Key words and phrases:

Kavannah: a mantra, comprised of a small unit of sacred text

If you want to know more:

Nan Fink Gefen, *Discovering Jewish Meditation: A Beginner's Guide to an Ancient Spiritual Practice*. Woodstock, VT: Jewish Lights Publishing, 1999.
Aryeh Kaplan, *Jewish Meditation: A Practical Guide*. New York: Schocken Books, 1995.

More particulars:

Before you go to sleep each night, follow the practice of Levi Yitzchak of Berditchev and take a *cheshbon hanefesh*, an accounting of the soul. Recall the name of anyone who may have wronged you during the day and as you recall his or her name, forgive that person and pray for his or her welfare. Then affirm the Oneness of God, your longing to be united with the Divine and then say the *Shema*. Finally, review all of your actions during the day. Start by taking only a few minutes to do this and increasing the amount of time devoted to this activity over time. Select one or two actions in which you believe that you acted wrongly and humbly ask God to help you remove this kind of action from your daily life.

Make a *Havdalah* Kit

The source:

If the Sabbath is to be remembered, then its departure must be noted.

What you need to know:

1. At approximately 42 minutes after sunset on Saturday evening (which is 25 hours after candle lighting on Friday evening), *havdalah* is made at the conclusion of *maariv*. Some wait 72 minutes. For many Jews, particularly among the Orthodox, 60 minutes after sunset is the norm or after three stars can be seen in the sky.

2. All you need is a candle made of up at least two separate wicks, preferably more; a full cup of wine (or grape juice); and a small container (referred to as a spice box) for spices (like cloves or cinnamon) or flowers. Put this together in a container or sack and pack it to take with you whenever you will be out-of-town for Shabbat. You can purchase small "single-size" bottles of grape juice for just such a purpose. (It also makes a nice "care package" for kids away at camp or college.)

Things to remember:

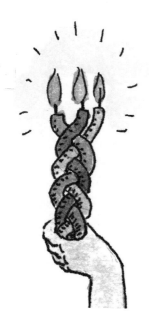

1. *Havdalah* is a ceremony that marks the transition between special time (like Shabbat and the holidays) and regular time (like ordinary days of the week). *Havdalah* prayers are also included during the *maariv* service itself, during the *Amidah*.

2. The order of *havdalah* is simple: introductory paragraph; wine (blessing but no drinking yet); spices (blessing then sniff); fire (blessing then we extend our hands toward the flame in order to see its reflection in our fingernails); then the final *havdalah* blessing (we drink the wine and then extinguish the flame in it). [If you use brandy—which is a wine—instead of regular wine, it will usually go aflame when the candle is set to it. If you are careful, this adds a lovely ending to the ritual.]

Key words and phrases:

Besamim: spices

Havdalah: a distinction or something that has been made separate

Ner havdalah: a *havdalah* candle, usually twisted to emphasize the mingling of the sacredness of Shabbat with the routine of the everyday

Shavuah tov: a good week; greetings extended to one another at the conclusion of *havdalah*

If you want to know more:

Ronald H.Isaacs, *Shabbat Delight: A Celebration in Stories, Games, and Songs*. Hoboken, NJ and New York: KTAV Publishing and the American Jewish Committee, 1987.

Kerry Olitzky and Ronald Isaacs, *The "How to" Handbook for Jewish Living*, Vol. 1. Hoboken, NJ: KTAV Publishing, 1993.

More particulars:

1. When a holiday falls on weekday, there are certain changes to be made in the *havdalah* ritual. The introductory verses, candle and spices are omitted. At the conclusion of Yom Kippur, when it does not coincide with Shabbat, the introductory verses and the spices are omitted. However, the blessing over the flame is recited from a candle that has been lit with a fire that had been burning throughout Yom Kippur. According to traditional Jewish law, if one is not available, then the blessing over the flame is omitted.

2. *Havdalah* is said standing or sitting, depending on the custom of the community. Most people stand for it. If *havdalah* is made in the synagogue, in some communities the first paragraph is omitted.

3. Since you cease from creation during Shabbat, lighting the candle as the first act following Shabbat indicates that you have re-entered the creative mode. According to a midrash, fire was created on the first Saturday night (see Babylonian Talmud, *Pesachim* 54a).

4. We use spices (a symbol of the spiritual pleasures of Shabbat) to enliven our senses once the extra soul that we gain during Shabbat is gone and to raise our spirits following the departure of the Sabbath queen.

5. Most people sing a *shavuah tov* song at the end of the ceremony, following the singing of *Eliahu Hanavi*.

Move Toward Greater Shabbat Observance

The source:

"Remember the Sabbath day and keep it holy" (Exodus 20:8).

What you need to know:

1. Assess your current pattern of observance (or non-observance) of Shabbat. What do you do on Friday night, Saturday morning and afternoon? Then choose what will be easiest to change. Leave the hard things for last. For example, it will probably be easiest to transform Friday night dinner into a family Shabbat dinner if you already get together as a family for that dinner. Take it slowly. One thing at a time. Make a list of what changes you plan on doing and how quickly you think you can integrate them into your life. Some things will take longer than others. Begin simply by moving your Friday night dinner from the kitchen into the dining room. Put a table cloth on the table. Set it with flowers. Start the meal with blessings (wine or grape juice; *challah*). Bless your children and speak words of praise to a spouse. Review the week with those assembled at the table, but stay away from discussing challenges at work that require resolution. And avoid any discussions about money and finance. And don't forget to intersperse the courses with song—much better than intermezzo sorbet! At the end of the meal, express your gratitude to God for the food on the table and the friends and family with whom you are sharing it. When you are ready, use *birkat hamazon* at the end of the meal. Start with the short version, then add elements in the weeks following.

2. Next, focus on your preparation for Shabbat. When do you begin? How do you plan ahead? Then, determine a routine for Friday afternoon. Leave work early. Be conscious of doing errands on time, such as picking

up last-minute things that you will need. Take a shower. Change your clothes. Dress in things that you don't wear from day to day.

3. For some people, it is easier to start Friday evenings by going to the synagogue. For others, it makes more sense to *daven* at home rather than rush to a late-night service.

4. Turn off the telephone—or let the answering machine pick it up. People will soon realize that Shabbat is not the time to call you. And you don't want to be bothered by solicitations in any case. And leave the TV and radio off, as well. Let the natural sounds entertain you one day a week. And stay out of the shopping malls and away from the movie theaters. Instead use this time of leisure to read or study.

5. Begin your Saturday at the synagogue. Go early and stay for the entire service. Luxuriate in the fact that you don't have to rush off to go anywhere. Come home for a leisurely meal. Invite your friends to join you. (Shabbat is always nicer when you share it with others.) After this lunch has become part of the routine (even the menu does not vary much in our home), then you may want to introduce some more traditional elements into it, such as table blessings and songs. (Don't forget *kiddush* wine and *challah* for this meal too.)

6. Next comes the best part of Shabbat: a nap, something that we anticipate with as much enthusiasm and longing as we do the more potentially ethereal aspects of Shabbat such as prayer and study. One would think that you can easily add this into your Shabbat schedule, but it is not so easy. Shabbat naps are only possible when demands are not being made on the rest of your time.

7. Following your nap, it should be time for *mincha*. Just as this service is the most challenging in our daily routine (even if it is the simplest and least complicated) since we are in the midst of other things and have to break away from them in order to *daven mincha*, it is hard to return to the synagogue in the afternoon. That is why some synagogues schedule *mincha*

either after the *kiddush* following morning services (within the parameters set forward by Jewish law) or just before *maariv* and *havdalah* in the evening. Usually, some study separates the two services, regardless of whether it is held early or late in the afternoon. However, some communities use the reading of the Torah on Saturday afternoon for study. Late afternoon/early evening is a particularly nice time in the summer to study, since sunset is much later than it is the rest of the year. And the third *shabbat meal* (called *seudah shlishit* in Hebrew or *shalosh seudos* in Yiddish) which is usually lighter fare is eaten between *mincha* and *maariv*.

For some, it is easier to get into the routine of Shabbat *mincha* by *davening* at home. For others, it is easier to establish the routine by joining with the community at prayer.

8. At the end of Shabbat, gather together and bid it farewell. This is accomplished ritually in *havdalah*. While the ceremony is rather brief, and people are often in a hurry to go out on Saturday night, feel free to add other elements into the ritual. For example, share with one another your plans for the week ahead, the challenges you face, or what you would like to accomplish.

9. This is the time of Shabbat that is often most difficult. That is why *havdalah* is bittersweet. We want to re-enter secular time, but we hesitate to leave holy time behind. What is even more difficult for those of us who live in mixed communities is the fact that during the summer when Shabbat ends around 9 p.m., our friends may not be willing to wait for us to go out. That's why it is important to try to develop relationships with those who are on the path to their own renewal of Jewish observance, rather than compromising your own Shabbat observance to meet the social needs of your friends. Once you change this rhythm and you let Shabbat become embedded in your soul, none of this will seem strange to you. What may seem strange instead is going to the movies on a late Friday afternoon, early evening in the summer since Shabbat begins—as it ends—very late.

Things to remember:

1. Shabbat is not a burden. Its goal is the exact opposite: to ease the burdens of daily living by making them unimportant one day a week. It is an opportunity to bring joy and tranquility into your life by collapsing ancient time (of Paradise) with future (messianic) time and thereby making time as we know it irrelevant.

2. People observe Shabbat in various ways regardless of the particular community in which they live. Once you have determined the community of religious observance in which you feel most comfortable, use the observance patterns of others to guide you, but do not use what they do as a measuring stick for what you have chosen for your own life, and the life of your family.

3. You will not be able to recreate the pattern of observance of your parents or grandparents—if they had one. Instead, you must create your own, one that feels comfortable for you and helps to create Jewish memories for your children, as it affirms your own. Be creative. Be open.

Key words and phrases:

Birkat hamazon: grace after meals
Challah: special bread, twisted like the braids of the hair of the mystical Sabbath bride
Daven: pray
Havdalah: ritual that marks the separation between Shabbat and the rest of the week
Kiddush: prayer of sanctification said over wine
Maariv: evening service
Mincha: afternoon service

If you want to know more:

Ronald H.Isaacs, *Shabbat Delight: A Celebration in Stories, Games, and Songs*. Hoboken, NJ and New York: KTAV Publishing and the American Jewish Committee, 1987.
Kerry M. Olitzky and Ronald H. Isaacs, *Sacred Celebrations: A Jewish Holiday Handbook*. Hoboken, NJ: KTAV Publishing Co., 1994.

More particulars:

1. Because of the impact of Jewish law on our routine as we usher in Shabbat and bid it farewell (through *havdalah*), Shabbat is actually 25 hours long. It begins approximately 18 minutes before sunset on Friday and concludes when there are three stars evident in the sky on Saturday evening (or 42 minutes after sunset). Shabbat does not begin or end when you are ready.

2. "More than Israel has kept the Sabbath, has the Sabbath kept Israel." (Ahad Ha-am)

Observe *Yom Hashoah*

The source:

A resolution of the Knesset, Israel's national legislature, on April 12, 1951 designated the 27th of Nisan as "Holocaust and Ghetto Uprising Day, a day of perpetual remembrance for the House of Israel."

What you need to know:

1. Yom Hashoah marks the anniversary of the Holocaust. While there are those who believe that its observance should be part of Tisha B'av, most members of the Jewish community have fixed it on their calendars.

2. Yom Hashoah has become more of a public community observance than a personal observance. However, of late, introduced by the Federation of Men's Clubs of the Conservative movement (United Synagogue of Conservative Judaism), many people light yellow candles that function in much the same way as *yahrzeit* candles (that burn for 24 hours). Some people light six candles (white or yellow) in order to acknowledge the six million of our people who perished.

3. Since this is a day like no other, find some time for yourself to reflect on the tragedy of the Holocaust. Take a few moments to think about those in your family who perished. Study in their memory. Give *tzedakah* in their memory. Teach in their memory.

Things to remember:

1. In the synagogue, the observance of Yom Hashoah is usually held in combination with the evening service. Candles are lit and special prayers such as *El Maleh Rachamim* and *kaddish* are added. Holocaust poems and literature are often read and public testimony by survivors is usually offered. Songs of the partisans may be sung (often in Yiddish, the Jewish folk language that was nearly destroyed in the Holocaust along with the people who spoke it). And the *ani ma'amin* prayer

is generally sung in a dirge-like melody that was sung by the victims of the Holocaust often as they were marched to their deaths.

Key words and phrases:

Shoah: holocaust, literally "conflagration by fire"
Yahrzeit: anniversary of one's death

If you want to know more:

Kerry M. Olitzky and Ronald H. Isaacs, *Sacred Celebrations: A Jewish Holiday Handbook*. Hoboken, NJ: KTAV Publishing Co., 1994.

More particulars:

1. Yom Hashoah is observed a week before Yom Haatzmaut, in order to emphasize the fact that the Jewish people emerged from the ashes of the Holocaust in order to build the modern state of Israel.

2. Outside Israel, in the early years of the observance, it was customary to memorialize the Holocaust on April 19, the day on which the Warsaw Ghetto uprising began.

3. The tenth of Tevet was designated by the Israeli Chief Rabbinate as the day of *yahrzeit* for *kaddish* to be said by relatives of those who had lost family in the Holocaust and who did not know the exact day they perished.

Personalize a Bar/Bat Mitzvah

The source:

At 13, one is ready for the *mitzvot* (Pirke Avot 5:23).

What you need to know:

1. Bar/Bat Mitzvah is not something that is bestowed on you or something that you do. It is a state of being that is determined by your age. Once boys become 13 or girls become 12 (though most non-Orthodox congregations no longer make a distinction of age between boys and girls), according to their birthdays as reckoned by the Hebrew calendar, you gain certain privileges in the community. With these privileges, you also incur certain responsibilities. This time of transition from childhood—where these privileges and obligations had no impact on you—and adulthood is marked by the most salient of these privileges, that is, the right to be called to the Torah for an *aliyah*.

2. As you think about personalizing your bar/bat mitzvah, make sure that it enhances the ceremony and celebration (and thereby becomes *hiddur mitzvah*) and neither eclipses it or replaces it in importance. That is why it is important that the process of personalization emerge out of Jewish tradition. For example, since the *haftarah* reading is supposed to be educational (unlike the Torah reading which is primarily intended to simulate the experience at Sinai) and highlight the theme of the Torah reading, you may want to narrate the *haftarah* reading for those in the congregation. Place it in context. Help people to understand what is being read and why it is being read and how it really relates to the Torah reading. As another option, particularly for those unfamiliar with the service, you may want to provide a guide and commentary to the service. These can be distributed with the prayer books as people enter the synagogue. Similarly, you may want to distribute something ahead of time that helps visitors to understand what is so important about the ceremony they will be attending. This is more than rules and regulations for guests to the syn-

agogue. This is about what the ceremony means to you and your family and how you prepared for it.

3. There are many things that are now common in many synagogues that may need rethinking if you want to personalize the ceremony and make it more meaningful to you. What will you do with the flowers that are placed on the *bimah*—if they are there at all? If there is a reception or *kiddush*, will people be invited to donate to *tzedakah* the equivalent of what they might have spent had they paid for the meal? Or alternatively, will the leftover food be given (within the bounds of local health department standards) to a local "feed the hungry" program? Perhaps you may want to consider identifying a charitable cause that you can champion (or already have) so that people can provide funds in your honor to the organization. Make sure that you include information on the organization either in the invitation or on the day itself.

Things to remember:

1. Each community has its parameters with regard to bar/bat mitzvah, as well as worship in general. Make sure that you review with your rabbi what options are available to you. Plan well in advance since some of these things may have to be reviewed by the congregation's ritual committee. The bar/bat mitzvah is placed in the context of regular community worship. The challenge, therefore, is to personalize the bar/bat mitzvah in such a way that it does not compromise the experience of worship for the community.

2. Review what responsibilities and obligations, rights and privileges accrue to the bar/bat mitzvah in your community. After you decide how to personally respond to these, you will then be able to develop a more complete plan for personalizing the bar/bat mitzvah.

Key words and phrases:

Aliyah: Torah honor, may also refer to immigrating to Israel
Bar: son, from the Aramaic
Bat: daughter
Bimah: raised platform at the front of the synagogue

Hiddur mitzvah: beautifying the mitzvah
Mitzvah: commandment, sacred obligation

If you want to know more:

Ronald Isaacs, *Reaching for Sinai: A Practical Handbook for Bar/Bat Mitzvah and Family*. Hoboken, NJ: KTAV Publishing, 1989.

Jeffrey Salkin, *For Kids—Putting God on the Guest List: How to Claim the Spiritual Meaning of Your Bar or Bat Mitzvah*. Woodstock, VT: Jewish Lights Publishing, 1999.

———, *Putting God on the Guest List: How to Reclaim the Spiritual Meaning of Your Child's Bar or Bat Mitzvah*. Woodstock, VT: Jewish Lights Publishing, 1992.

Plan a Spiritual Trip to Israel

The source:

God said to Abram, "Raise your eyes and look out from where you are, to the north and south, to the east and west, for I give you all the land that you see, to you and your ancestors forever" (Gen. 13: 14–15).

What you need to know:

1. Use a layered approach to your trip, what Rabbi Larry Hoffman labels as "anticipate, approach, acknowledge, and afterthought."

   A. Anticipate: once you have determined where you want to go, spend some time thinking about the place. Read a little about it in history, but don't get bogged down. Just get a feel for the place and what happened there.

   B. Approach: since you are coming as a pilgrim to the site, prepare yourself accordingly, maybe a poem, a prayer. Think about the way you should dress, as well.

   C. Acknowledge: Once you have arrived, take note of the place. Don't rush for photo opportunities. Simply drink in the environment. Say a blessing. Study a bit of Torah or repeat something that you have learned and share it with others. This is about spiritual feelings, not facts and figures.

   D. Afterthought: How do you keep the experience alive? Some people like to write things down in a journal. This is not "what I did on my summer vacation." Instead, write down what you felt, the smells, the sounds and the sights. Bits of conversation that you might have heard, even something simple like children playing outside and the sound of their laughter and the sweetness of their innocent voices.

Things to remember:

1. Plan well in advance but be flexible enough so that you are open to spontaneous experiences while you are in Israel. Start your trip even before you leave. Ask your rabbi for an *aliyah* to the Torah prior to making your trip (and remember to *bentsch gomel* when you return safely, please God). Then make sure that you say *tefillat haderekh* once you get situated on the airplane. Add your own prayers to those that have been stipulated by our tradition. You are going home as a pilgrim to the land, not a tourist.

2. Bring a *siddur* and *tanakh* with you with which you are familiar and comfortable. Bring a map of Israel that is easy to read and highlights the places that you want to visit.

3. Be realistic about what you will be able to accomplish in the number of days that you plan on being in Israel and the often competing demands of those with whom you are traveling.

4. Use your trip to Israel as a way of trying out things like daily prayer and daily study that you will want to incorporate into your routine when you return home. Start slowly, perhaps with a daily psalm or one of the fixed prayer services and work your way toward a more extensive routine. Choose those experiences that speak directly to you out of the experience of our tradition. For example, beginning your first day in Israel by saying the daily blessings brings that memory with their recitation each time you say them.

5. Much of the trip will be about how you visit, rather than where you visit. Even breathing the crisp morning air in Jerusalem while walking through its streets can be a spiritual experience. It certainly is for us!

6. Don't try to read too much about the sites you will be visiting. Try to read one thing about each place that you want to remember. Then carry that with you as a kind of sacred mantra, a *kavannah*, for that particular place.

Key words and phrases:

Bentsch gomel: blessing after having survived a traumatic
    event, such as travel
Eretz Yisrael: the land of Israel
Tefillat haderekh: traveler's prayer

If you want to know more:

Lawrence A. Hoffman, *Israel, A Spiritual Travel Guide: A
    Companion for the Modern Jewish Pilgrim*. Woodstock,
    VT: Jewish Lights Publishing, 1998.

Pray with *Kavannah*

The source:

Babylonian Talmud, *Berakhot* 13a.

What you need to know:

1. Schedule for yourself enough time to pray. If you are more focused on the time you have to conclude your prayer, then it will be difficult for you to find the *kavannah* with which to pray.

2. Find a comfortable place for prayer, one that is pleasant but whose aesthetic will not be distracting. Try to avoid influencing the senses, particularly with any background noises, except perhaps those of nature.

3. Be conscious of the way you are dressed for prayer. Your mode of dress helps you with the way you feel about prayer and approach it.

4. Take it slowly. The goal of prayer is not how much you can say and how fast you can say it. (Avoid what we like to call "mumble-*davening*.") This is particularly true with the preliminary material in a formal service such as *pesuke d'zimra*. These "verses of song," as they are called, are supposed to be just that. So choose a verse in a psalm that speaks to you and repeat it over and over again until you are able to transcend the words themselves. Let them imprint themselves on your soul so that you can carry their lingering memory throughout the day. Let them be the prism through which you experience the world around you. Sing the verse aloud if you know a particular melody for it. Don't feel obligated to rush through the entire psalm, nor each and every one of them in the prayer book. The goal of prayer is to create a pathway through which your prayers can reach God and open up the dialogue with the Divine.

5. Don't be afraid to use your body in prayer. When we are lucky, community prayer breaks into dance (such as on Erev Shabbat). But *shukeling* (swaying) also reflects the rhythm of Jewish prayer. People *shukel* dur-

ing prayer in much the same way as they tap their feet to music. It is the way we keep in tune with the prayers. It also serves to disorient ourselves from regular space and enter into the space of prayer. Try it. Don't be too self-critical and certainly don't be critical of others who do. And please don't assign certain prayer movements to specific groups of Jews. All of Jewish tradition, custom, and ritual is ours to embrace.

Things to remember:

1. *Kavannah* is more about the attitude with which we pray, rather than the words of prayer themselves. Some people even think that the words are irrelevant, as long as the heart and soul are directed to Heaven.

2. Don't confuse being an expert in liturgy with being able to pray with *kavannah*. Sometimes, a lot of knowledge gets in the way when we confuse prayer with liturgy. And sometimes we get in our own way when we worry about how much we do not know, or how inadequate is our Hebrew. You can also pray in English (but don't deceive yourself into believing that translating makes the praying any easier or that responsive readings are prayers).

3. Leave your critical self at the door. Prayer is a meta-rational experience.

4. Leave your burdens of the day at the door, as well. Try to shake off any residual memory of yesterday's challenges and try not to enter into today's challenges either. If you have had any recent arguments with those you love, try to bring them to closure before you pray. Sometimes a simple "I'm sorry" is all that it takes.

Key words and phrases:

Kavannah: the sacred intention with which one prays; the technical term for spontaneous prayer (in distinction to the *keva* of fixed prayer); a mantra of sorts made up of words or texts, primarily of sacred origin
Keva: fixed prayer, the daily routine of prayer
Pesuke d'zimra: verses of song, from the morning service

If you want to know more:

Yitzchak Buxbaum, *Real Davening*. Flushing, NY: Jewish Spiritual Booklet Series, 1996.

Lawrence A. Hoffman, *The Art of Public Prayer*. Woodstock, VT: Jewish Lights Sky Paths Publishing, 1999.

_____, *My People's Prayer Book* series. Woodstock, VT: Jewish Lights Publishing, 1997ff.

Ellen Singer, ed., *Paradigm Shift: The Jewish Renewal Teachings of Reb Zalman Schachter-Shalomi*. Northvale, NJ: Jason Aronson, 1993. (See section on *Davvenology*.)

More particulars:

Some people find that using sign language during prayer helps them to find the right posture for their prayers. Find someone in your community that can help you sign those prayers that you find are pivotal to your experience of worship.

Start a Study *Chavurah*

The source:

"Get a study buddy" (*Pirke Avot* 1:6).

"The study of Torah is equal to them all (that is, *mitzvot* that have no specific measure), because it leads to them all" (Mishnah *Peah* 1:1, also included in the *siddur*).

What you need to know:

1. To begin, a good-sized group should be about 12 people. This allows for some flexibility should people not be able to attend each session.

2. While no one should be in charge, it is sometimes helpful for an individual to chair each meeting. We recommend a rotating chairperson. This person would be responsible for planning and guiding the study session in any given week. But the responsibility of leading the group remains in the hands of the entire group. Since this is a peer group, it is important that each person take an equal role in it.

3. Choose a subject that you think will be of interest to people. You may want to begin with the weekly Torah or Haftarah reading or you may want to choose a classic of sacred literature such as *Pirke Avot* since it is easily accessible. As an alternative, books like *Sefer Hakhinukh* (lit. Book of Education, a book of mitzvah education) or *Mesillat Yesharim* (a classic work on ethical piety) are excellent choices for groups and are available in English translation. You may also want to consult Michael Katz and Gershon Schwartz, *Swimming in the Sea of Talmud* (Philadelphia: Jewish Publication Society, 1997).

4. Invite two friends to participate. And ask them to invite two of their friends and so on until you have a group of 12 people.

5. At the outset, don't be too democratic. As the founder of the group, you can make certain logistical decisions

until the group takes shape. Be sensitive to the needs of others, but choose the venue, the time for the first meeting, etc.

6. Be clear about the expectations from the beginning. If this is to be a group that only studies when it meets, then be sure that everyone knows that. However, if members of the group want a more extensive study experience and are willing to study independently at times when the group is not meeting, then that has to be made clear to potential group members, as well.

7. Start each session with the blessing for the study of Torah as a way of reminding the participants of the sacred nature of Jewish study. *Barukh ata Adonai Elohenu Melekh Ha-olam asher kidshanu bemitzvotav vitzivanu la'asok bidivrei Torah.* "Praised are You, Adonai our God, Sovereign of the Universe who makes us holy with *mitzvot* and instructs us to busy ourselves with the words (and works) of Torah."

Things to remember:

1. In a study group, everyone is equal even if some of its members have certain Hebrew or text skills or background that are superior to others.

2. The group should meet on a regular basis so that it is something that its members can fit into their regular routine and they come to expect it.

3. It is good to build into your study *chavurah* a Jewish calendar rhythm so that its nuances can be included in your study.

4. A study group can begin with two people committed to study.

5. Depending on when you meet, include the routine of *tefillah* in your meetings.

6. Try to make a schedule of your subject matter, but let the learning lead you. Some people prefer to use the weekly Torah portion as a guide. Others choose to start at Genesis and then just keep going.

7. Take note of all practical considerations:

a. Where should the meeting take place?
b. Will the meeting schedule accommodate all who are invited to participate?
c. Is there room for more people to join as the group evolves?
d. Does everyone have transportation?

Key words and phrases:

Chavurah: fellowship (surrogate extended family)
Chevruta: study partner; study buddy
Talmud torah: classical Jewish study

If you want to know more:

Sharon Strassfeld and Michael Strassfeld, *The Third Jewish Catalogue*. Philadelphia: Jewish Publication Society of America, 1980.

Talk to Your Kids About God

The source:

"I am Adonai Your God who brought you out of the land of Egypt, out of the house of bondage. You shall worship only Me" (Exodus 20:1–2).

What you need to know:

1. Make sure that you have provided an open environment in which your children feel comfortable in talking to you about God (or anything else, for that matter).

2. Since most people think that Godtalk is closely related to patterns of religious observance, it is important for your children to realize that their relationship to God is not limited to the confines of their religious school classroom or the synagogue (that you may have chosen not to attend very frequently).

3. Children take their cues from what they hear and what they observe more than what we tell them.

4. While no one is certain about their relationship to God, it will be important for you to reflect on your own feelings before talking with your children. You may want to begin by talking with your spouse or an intimate friend. (Sometimes it is helpful for older children to speak to younger children.)

5. Begin these conversations while they are young. Let them evolve from their experiences with God and the world rather than a decision that you may have made that it is time to talk about God. Also, this allows God to be discussed in the context of an experience with the Divine rather than limited to merely an intellectual discussion. You may want to read books together that provide a viewpoint on God for your child to understand in order to foster such a conversation.

6. Help them to understand something that many of our rabbis and cantors don't fully understand: that heartfelt prayer should be the foundation for worship. However, prayer should not be limited to the words in

the prayer book. It should be an expression of our hearts and souls.

7. Finally, our understanding of God grows as we grow, as we experience attributes of the Divine in our own lives. It is a dynamic understanding and a dynamic relationship.

Things to remember:

1. Be honest. Share your struggles and your doubts as your children are ready to understand them. Admit to inconsistencies, as well. And invite them to join you on a journey of exploration.

2. Remember that most children cannot think abstractly. That is why the narrative material in the Torah speaks so vividly to them in concrete terms. Don't dismiss these stories as primitive myths.

3. Because of the covenant between God and the Jewish people (and therefore with each of us), we are never alone. Our obligation is to live a life reflective of that covenant.

4. Don't try to tell your children everything at once.

5. Even if your posture is rational with little room for the metarational, don't rob your children of the mystery that a relationship with God can offer.

6. Don't confuse your experience with God with the ways in which your children might experience God.

Key words and phrases:

Adonai: the conventional euphemism used for the unspeakable name (the tetragrammaton) of the personal God of Israel

Elohim: the way the Torah generally speaks of God in abstract terms.

If you want to know more:

Ronald Isaacs, *Close Encounters: Jewish Views About God*. Northvale, NJ: Jason Aronson, 1996.

Harold Kushner, *When Children Ask About God*. New York: Schocken Books, 1971.

David Wolpe, *Teaching Your Children About God*. New York: HarperTrade, 1994.

More particulars:

In an essay entitled, "Talking to Kids About God," Rabbi Daniel Syme offers these guidelines for parents:

1. Do not offer the biblical notion of God—or any one concept—as "the" Jewish God idea.

2. When you speak to your children about God, state your personal beliefs, but clearly indicate that they are *your* beliefs.

3. Use appropriate language when discussing God with children of younger ages.

4. When your child volunteers a personal notion as to the nature of God, try to tie that affirmation to a great Jewish thinker.

5. Never be embarrassed to respond, "I don't know" to a child's question about God.

6. Do not hesitate to consult with your rabbi, Jewish educator, or others to deal with difficult questions.

7. Encourage your children to share their thoughts about God and instances when they feel they have experienced God in their lives.

8. Listen better.

9. Emphasize to your children that our personal ideas of God grow as we grow, both in depth and in complexity.

10. Help your child see ritual, prayer, and holiday observances as ways in which the Jewish people express their attachment to God.

11. Do not be reluctant to share stories of times in your life when you experienced or felt close to God.

Use the Book of Psalms

The source:

Jewish custom.

What you need to know:

1. Keep a book of psalms handy. Some people keep a copy in their briefcases or purses, as well as on the table next to their bed. In this way, they can access the psalms easily, review them when they awaken in the morning (in order to help start the day) and reflect on them at night (to help them reflect on the day that just passed).

2. Read each psalm that you have chosen slowly. Focus on one verse or even one word.

Things to remember:

1. People read psalms at various times in their lives. Such reading helps people focus and offers direction, particularly in time of need. The reading of psalms can raise the spirit when it is low or offer direction and insight when one feels lost or misguided. The reading of psalms takes place when a body is being watched over following death. A traditional groom recites psalms while his bride makes the circuit around him. Psalms are said for people to bring them healing. And they have found their way in whole or in part throughout Jewish liturgy.

2. The service called *kabbalat Shabbat*, which grew out of the mystical tradition in Judaism, includes a series of psalms. One is supposed to reflect on the past week, one day at a time, as each psalm is read.

Key words and phrases:

Kabbalat Shabbat: service for welcoming Shabbat that precedes the Shabbat evening service
Tehillim: psalms

If you want to know more:

Yitzchak Buxbaum, *Jewish Spiritual Practices*. Northvale,
    NJ: Jason Aronson, 1994.
Simkha Y. Weintraub, ed. *Healing of Soul, Healing of Body:
    Spiritual Leaders Unfold the Strength and Solace in Psalms.*
    Woodstock, VT: Jewish Lights Publishing, 1994.

More particulars:

1. Rabbi Nachman of Bratslav designated these psalms as
    psalms for healing for what he called a *tikkun klali*, a
    complete remedy: 16, 32, 41, 42, 59, 77, 90, 105, 137,
    150.

2. The twenty-third psalm is well-known for its ability to
    provide comfort. Therefore, it is associated with
    mourning.

3. Just as there are many translations of the Bible, there
    are many translations of the various books in the
    Bible, including the book of Psalms. Since all transla-
    tion is interpretation, you may find that one transla-
    tion of a particular psalm speaks to you differently
    than does another translation.

4. Many psalms speak to people in different ways. After
    you become more familiar with individual psalms,
    you may find that you resonate with each one differ-
    ently depending on the context in which you are
    reciting a particular one. Start with these (feel free to
    copy this list and place it inside your own book of
    Psalms)[1]

    a. When studying Torah: 1, 19, 119
    b. In the synagogue: 5, 26, 27, 63, 65, 73, 84, 96,
        122, 135
    c. In nature: 19, 104, 148
    d. Desire to repent: 40, 51, 90
    e. After committing sin: 25, 32, 51, 130
    f. Sad, depressed: 30, 42, 43
    g. Cannot sleep: 4

[1]Adapted from Yitzchak Buxbaum, *Jewish Spiritual Practices*. Northvale, NJ: Jason Aronson, 1994, p. 366.

h. Lonely: 25

i. Disruptive changes in your life; personal tragedy: 46, 57

j. Frustration at the evil of people: 36, 52, 53, 58

k. Anxiety from those who seek to do you harm: 3, 5, 6, 7, 9, 17, 22, 25, 31, 35, 38, 43, 54, 55, 56, 57, 59, 71, 140, 142

l. Anxious concern about livelihood: 23, 62, 68

m. Suffering, afflicted: 38, 102

n. Want to pray, say psalms, speak to God: 51

o. Need to increase your trust in God: 22, 23, 56, 62, 84, 123, 125, 128, 131, 146

p. Single, hoping to find soulmate: 68

q. Feeling uplifted: 8, 19, 24, 47, 48

r. Need God's help, protection: 70, 91, 121, 130

s. Confused by success of wicked, envious of rich: 1, 37, 49, 73

t. Beset by the challenges of old age: 71

u. Perplexed by injustice and God's distance: 10

v. Doubts about faith: 1, 2, 19, 37

w. Feeling confused about your faith: 25, 143

x. Israel, Jews, Judaism pressed, abused, threatened: 53, 74, 83, 124

y. Betrayed, hurt by others, particularly someone close to you: 35, 41, 55

z. Feel abandoned: 27, 88, 142

aa. Feeling of thankfulness to God: 9, 18, 65, 66, 116

bb. Grateful to God for success, prosperity: 65, 144, 147

cc. Feel threatened, anxious or afraid: 4, 22, 23, 56

dd. Slandered, abused verbally, victim of wrongdoing: 39, 64, 120

ee. Great troubles and distress: 6, 31, 34, 55, 69, 77, 86, 88, 107, 121, 138, 142

ff. Feel humiliated by people: 22

Choose a Religious School

The source:

"You shall teach them diligently to your children" (Deuteronomy 6:7).

What you need to know:

1. There are several important questions that concerned parents ought to be thinking about when choosing a school for their child:

   a. When should we begin our child's Jewish education?
   b. What is the right kind of school for our child?
   c. How do we decide among schools of different sponsorships—private, communal, denominational, congregational?
   d. What if there is only one school available in our community? Do we still have options?

2. It is important to enroll early, as early as preschool and primary programs. Before enrolling in such programs, consider the goals of the school and whether they coincide with your own. Don't be persuaded by the reputation of the school in the community. Check it out yourself. And trust your "gut."

3. Although no single factor can account for the effectiveness or so-called "quality" of any school, here are some guidelines you may wish to look for when choosing a Jewish school.

Characteristics of Effective Schools

What Parents should look for when choosing a religious school

Well-defined philosophy and mission
> Ask to see a copy of school's goals and mission statement.

A system of evaluation to frequently monitor student progress
> Look for ways in which school determines whether

students are learning what school is teaching (achievement tests, report cards, etc.).

Sequential curriculum that matches philosophy
Does school have written curriculum that lists teachers' goals and student objectives for each grade?

School climate and plant
Tour the school and see if you can be given a chance to see school in action.
Is the school environment conducive for learning?

Strong educational director
Meet and get to know school principal.

Experienced teaching staff
Ask for information about teachers.
What are their backgrounds, teaching styles, etc?

Strong community support
Is there adequate financial support and advocacy for school in the community?

Things to remember:

1. Your ability to analyze a school assumes that there are options in the community. This is not always the case. Always keep in mind that the school should not represent the only option for Jewish education. It is just one of them. Jewish home experiences, camping experiences, and community and youth programs all contribute to one's Jewish education. One has to provide support for the other.

2. If you have a Jewish day school in your community, you will certainly want to learn more about it as a possibility for your children. Since there is a high correlation between the number of hours of Jewish education a child receives and the development of one's Jewish identity, the day school is more likely to provide a student with better resources for living a Jewish life. Day school education also means additional financial obligation. Most day schools also expect more parental involvement than do most congregational schools, especially in the area of fundraising and policy making.

More particulars:

1. Learning-disabled children are entitled to a Jewish education. Be an advocate in your community. Make sure that all children receive a Jewish education, according to their need and ability. *P'tach*, which stands for "**P**arents for **T**orah for **A**ll **C**hildren" is a national organization devoted to making sure that learning-disabled kids get a Jewish education. *P'tach* headquarters are located at 1363 49th Street, Brooklyn, NY 11219. There are branches all around North America, as well as in Israel.

2. Be aware of any challenges that your children face concerning their Jewish education. The earlier, the better.

Key words and phrases:

Bet Sefer: School
Bet Sefer Yomi: Day school

If you want to know more:

Hayim Halevy Donin, *To Raise a Jewish Child: A Guide for Parents*. New York: Basic Books, 1977.

Teach Civil Responsibility

The source:

"Do not separate yourself from the community" (*Pirke Avot* 2:5).

What you need to know:

1. Jewish teachers have always stressed responsible citizenship in the community in which one resides. The prophet Jeremiah (29:7) taught: "Seek the peace of the city where I have caused you to be carried away, and pray to God for it."

2. Since values and attitudes related to any ideology are initially formed in the home, show your own children that Jewish people care not only about the Jewish community but the community at large.

3. There are many windows of opportunity that Judaism provides for transmitting notions of civic responsibility. For example, the *mitzvah* of *tzedakah* (righteous giving) reminds us of our responsibility of reaching out to the needy. Use the *pushke* (charity box) each week and let all family members share in placing coins into it before Shabbat, the traditional time to do so. If there are marches for the hungry, food collections sponsored by local synagogues or your local Jewish Federation, or clothes drives for the needy, donate to them as a family. When children see parents reach into their pockets, they are immediately impressed with the value of giving to others.

4. As your children grow older you will want to encourage them to show that your family cares not only about Jewish concerns but concerns of the general community at large. Encourage your children to read and discuss both the daily newspaper and your local Jewish Federation's publication. At election time, have a family discussion related to the various candidates, and talk about which ones would be the best leaders based on their values of goodness and justice. Have your kids write letters to their leaders when they feel that a

particular wrong needs to be corrected. By reaching out as a family to all of those who are less fortunate than we, we can express the Jewish value of community—that all members are ultimately responsible for one another.

Key words and phrases:

Achrayoot ezrachee: Civic responsibility
Tzedakah: Righteous giving.

If you want to know more:

Kathy Green and Sharon Strassfeld, *The Jewish Family Book*. New York: Bantam Books, 1981.

Explain Death to Children

The source:

There is no classic source for this "How to."

What you need to know:

1. Children growing up today are more aware of death than most adults realize. They are confronted with it in TV, word and song, in the natural world of plants and animals, and among their friends and family.

2. Children may not understand what they see when they are ignored during the grieving process. Too often we heighten the child's feeling of isolation when we pretend that the loved one is still living.

3. A child's ability to understand the meaning of death and loss is dependent on his or her cognitive development and life experiences.

4. A child of two years of age can sense loss and suffer the feelings that go with that loss, but is not likely to comprehend death in an intellectual sense. Parents of children this age can respond to a child's feelings, but explanations are not likely to be of substantial value.

5. Children aged three or four tend to think of death as a temporary condition and view it as separation.

6. Children between ages five and nine are much better able to understand the meaning of physical death. At this age, they may begin to worry about the time when those close to them will no longer "exist."

7. By the time children are aged nine or ten, they begin to formulate more realistic conceptions of death based on biological observances and their wider experience of the world. They begin to understand that death is the final end of bodily life.

8. There is no one proper way to tell a child about death. Although what is said is significant, how it is said is also very important. Consider carefully the tone of your

voice and the context in which the information is being shared.

9. Don't overwhelm children with too much detail. Remember to keep in mind the child's level of comprehension.

10. Avoid theological abstractions and detailed explanations, so that death will not be linked to sin or divine punishment.

11. Avoid myths and fairy tales that will later have to be rejected (e.g., Grandpa went away on a long trip; God took Daddy because your father was so good that God wanted him; Grandma has just gone to sleep).

12. Allow children time to express themselves and ask questions. Also allow them to talk about their fears and anxieties.

13. It is useful to explain in advance to children who will be attending the funeral what the chapel might look like, where the casket will be placed, where the family will be sitting, what the rabbi might say. Make sure that a member of the family or a close relative or friend sits with the children.

Things to remember

Speak from the heart and from your own belief. Be direct and truthful, always guided by the age of the child. Answer the questions asked, as they are asked. Be supportive and understanding. And don't be afraid to say, "I just don't know. Perhaps we can find out together."

If you want to know more:

Earl Grollman, ed., *Explaining Death to Children*. Boston: Beacon Press, 1969.

_____, *Talking About Death: A Dialogue Between Parent and Child*. Boston: Beacon Press, 1990.

Honor the Memory of the Deceased

The source:

Code of Jewish Law, Orach Chayim 568:8; Yoreh Deah 402:12.

What you need to know:

1. While there are certain activities that are required by Jewish law for those in mourning that honor the memory of the deceased (such as *shiva*, *sheloshim*, twelve months, *yahrzeit*, *yizkor*), there are many opportunities to honor the memory of the deceased beyond these specific obligations.

2. According to traditional law, there are certain family members obligated to say *kaddish* in memory of the deceased. However, others may assume this obligation, particularly when there are none who are alive to say *kaddish* or who are unable to do so for other reasons. Jewish law requires a *minyan* to be present when *kaddish* is said. If a *minyan* is not present, mourners are urged to study in memory of the deceased. Thus, study becomes a model for honoring the memory of the one who has died.

3. Similarly, when one teaches something that he or she has learned from another, that person is obligated to recall the teacher's name publicly as if he or she were in the room. This is particularly important when something was learned from someone who is no longer living. In addition, when Torah is taught, it can be taught to honor the memory of another.

4. The giving of *tzedakah* which is customarily tied to the daily routine of fixed prayer (three times daily) is also a means through which one can honor the memory of the deceased. Among people of means, this is extended on a larger scale in the form of programs and projects and even buildings.

5. Acts of *gemilut chasadim* also honor the memory of the deceased, particularly when the work that they started is carried on.

Things to remember:

When a person is recalled in conversation by name, Jewish etiquette suggests adding the words, "may s/he rest in peace"or "of blessed memory." Another customary phrase to honor the deceased is "may his or her memory be a blessing."

Key words and phrases:

Alav hashalom: may peace be unto him
Aleha hashalom: may peace be unto her
Gemilut chasadim: loving acts of kindness
Sheloshim: first 30 days of mournng
Shiva: first seven days of mourning
Twelve months: also referred to as *yud-bet chodesh* (a way of saying "twelve months" in Hebrew), marks the first twelve months of mourning (sometimes observed as eleven months in some communities with regard to the recitation of *kaddish*)
Tzedakah: charitable giving
Yahrzeit: (called *anos*, among Sephardic Jews), anniversary of a death, marked by saying *kaddish* by mourners
Yizkor: memorial service, part of the holiday liturgy
Zikhrona livrakha: may her memory be a blessing
Zikhrono livrakha: may his memory be a blessing

If you want to know more:

Kerry M. Olitzky, *Grief in Our Seasons*. Woodstock, VT: Jewish Lights Publishing, 1998.
Ron Wolfson, *"A Time to Mourn, a Time to Comfort."* New York: Federation of Jewish Men's Clubs, 1993.

More particulars:

There are others ways to remember our loved ones. Consider making *tzedakah* contributions in their memory to scholarship and lecture funds that will perpetuate their name, particularly to a cause or organization in which they were active or interested.

Do an Unveiling

The source:

"Jacob set up a pillar on Rachel's grave" (Genesis 35:20).

What you need to know:

1. Gather at the graveside of the deceased.

2. Read a few psalms that offer comfort such as Psalms 23 and 121.

3. Offer a few words in memory of the deceased, something that you want him/her to be remembered for.

4. Remove the cloth covering the gravestone.

5. Read the inscription on the stone.

6. Chant *El Malei Rachamim*.

7. Recite mourner's *kaddish,* if a minyan is present. (Reform Judaism historically does not require the presence of a *minyan.* However, a growing number of Reform rabbis require it nonetheless.)

8. Encourage each person present to place a small stone on the grave marker. (Laying stones on monuments is a sign that someone has visited the cemetery and is thus an acknowledgment that the deceased is still loved and remembered.)

Things to remember:

1. There is no specific time to erect a grave marker. It has become customary to do so at the conclusion of the first year of mourning, but it can take place anytime after thirty days. Unveilings may take place whenever grave visitations in general are permissible.

2. The custom of the unveiling is a Western custom that has evolved over time. Since the tombstone is covered with a cloth by many non-Orthodox families in North America—when it is installed—it is taken off by the family during the service. This ritual has come to be called an unveiling.

3. This is not to be another funeral. It is appropriate for immediate family and close friends to be invited, however. Although a rabbi frequently officiates, it is a brief, uncomplicated ceremony that can easily be led by a member of the family.

Key words and phrases:

Bet chayim: lit., house of life; cemetery
Chevrah kaddisha: burial society
Matzevah: headstone or grave marker
Sheloshim: period marking the first 30 days of mourning, following and including *shiva*
Shiva: the first seven days of mourning
Yahrzeit: anniversary of a person's death (called *anos* among Sephardim), based on the Hebrew date

If you want to know more:

Ronald H. Isaacs and Kerry M. Olitzky, *A Jewish Mourner's Handbook*. Hoboken, NJ: KTAV Publishing House, 1991.

More particulars:

1. There are a variety of markings that people use on headstones. It is common among Ashkenazim, to write the Hebrew letters *peh-nun*, the initials for *poh nach* or "here rests." Sephardim often use the Hebrew letters *mem-kuf*, the initials for *matzevet kevurah* or "monument of the grave of." Underneath the inscription on the headstone, one often finds the Hebrew letters *tav-nun-tzadee-bet-heh* for *tehi nishmato/nishmatah tzerurah bitzeror ha-chayyim* or "May his/her soul be bound up in the bond of eternal life."

2. A descendant of the Levites may have a ewer carved over the inscription since Levites washed the priests' hands in the ancient Temple prior to the recitation of the priestly blessing. This is still done is some synagogues prior to the offering of the priestly blessing by descendants of the priests. This is called *duchanen*.

3. The stone of a descendant of the priests (*kohanim*) is often marked by the carving of hands raised in the priestly blessing.

Do a *Taharah*

The source:

"As one came so shall one go" (Ecclesiastes 5:5); *Kitzur Shulchan Arukh*, chapter 197.

What you need to know:

1. Before the deceased is placed into his/her coffin, the custom is to wash the body in a ritual known as a *taharah* (ritual purification). Those who perform this ritual are generally members of the Holy Burial Society, known as the *Chevra Kaddisha* or *Chevra Kavod Hamet*. Some congregations have made this function part of their Caring Committee (or other committee that looks out for the welfare of the congregation and its members).

2. This is a general outline of the procedure for doing *taharah*. (Note: the precise procedure may vary from one *Chevra Kaddisha* or community to another.)

   i. The purification rite of the *taharah* generally takes place in a specially designated room in a mortuary.

   ii. Before the *taharah* begins, if you are participating in the *taharah*, wash your hands three times using a utensil.

   iii. The body lies facing up during the entire *taharah* procedure.

   iv. Using a large container, wash the body in lukewarm water in the following order: head, neck, right side of body, left side of body. Raise the deceased and wash the back in a similar manner beginning with the right side and then the left.

   v. Clean the nails of the hands and feet thoroughly.

   vi. It is also customary among some communities to comb the hair of the deceased.

   vii. Wash your hands again and wash the body again with 24 quarts of water poured over the head, so that the water flows down over the entire body.

   viii. Move the deceased and place him or her on a dry sheet and wipe him or her dry.

77

ix. According to some communities, mix the white of a raw egg with a little wine or vinegar and then wash the head with the mixture.

x. Now dress the body with *tachrichim* (white linen shrouds), consisting of several garments. Place the *mitznefet* (head dress) on the head and draw it down to cover the head and neck. Extend the *michnasayim* (trousers) from the belly to the ankles and tie them by making three forms that are shaped to resemble the Hebrew letter *shin*, a symbol of *Shaddai* (Almighty God). Around the ankles, tie each foot with a band, but do not form any knots. The *ketonet* (chemise) has an opening at the top to be slipped over the head and sleeves for the arms. At the neck, knot the bands with bows to resemble the Hebrew letter *shin*. The *kittel* (upper garment) has sleeves for the arms; draw it over the body. Wind the *avnet* (belt) around the body three times over the *kittel*, Make sure that both ends are knotted over the belly with three bows in the shape of the Hebrew letter *shin*.

xi. Choose the *tallit* (prayer shawl) that the deceased wore while praying when he was alive. Place the body in the coffin and wrap the *tallit* around the body. Tear one of the *tzitzit* (fringes) from the *tallit*. Then wrap the *sovev* (linen) sheet around the head.

xii. Place broken pieces of earthenware and a handful of earth from Israel (put into a linen bag) into the casket before it is closed.

xiii. Ask forgiveness of the deceased and then close the casket.

Things to remember:

1. If the deceased died instantaneously through violence or accidents, and his/her body and garments were completely spattered with blood, no washing or *taharah* is performed. The body is placed in the casket without the clothes being removed, and a sheet is wrapped over the clothes.

2. The custom of dressing in plain linen shrouds was to

prohibit a family from showing off its wealth by dressing the deceased in fancy clothing.

Key words and phrases:

Chevra Kaddisha/Chevra Kavod Hamet: Holy Burial Society
Tachrichim: Burial shrouds
Taharah: Ritual purification
Met: Deceased

If you want to know more:

Maurice Lamm, *The Jewish Way in Death and Mourning*. New York: Jonathan David, 1969.

Seven Laws of Noah

The source:

Babylonian Talmud, *Sanhedrin* 56a.

What you need to know:

1. While non-Jews are obviously not required to keep the *mitzvot*, Jewish tradition holds that non-Jews are bound by seven laws. These laws (which are called the Noahide Laws) are presumed to date from the time of Noah who is considered to be a righteous gentile. There are six negative laws and one positive one:

   a. Not to deny God (for example, idolatry)
   b. Not to blaspheme God
   c. Not to murder
   d. Not to engage in incest, adultery, bestiality, or homosexuality.
   e. Not to steal
   f. Not to eat a limb torn from a living animal
   g. To set up courts to ensure obedience to the other six laws.

2. Judaism regards any non-Jew who keeps these laws as a righteous person who is guaranteed a place in the world-to-come.

3. The medieval philosopher/theologian Moses Maimonides believed that a non-Jew was regarded as righteous only if the non-Jewish person observed the laws, because Maimonides believed that God commanded them, as well.

Things to remember:

1. The seven Noahide laws constitute the standard by which Jews assess the morality of a non-Jewish society.

2. The Noahide laws represent a theory of universal religion, emphasizing good actions rather than right be-

lief, ethical living rather than creedal statements. They require only loyalty to a basic code of ethical conduct, and rest upon the recognition of a divine Creator.

More particulars:

Traditional Judaism rejects homosexuality. In recent years, this posture has come under attack by various Jewish movements and organizations. In 1972, the Reform movement (through its lay organization, the Union of American Hebrew Congregations) accepted a gay synagogue into its membership. Both Hebrew Union College–Jewish Institute of Religion, the rabbinical seminary of the Reform movement, and the Reconstructionist Rabbinical College have accepted gay members to study for the rabbinate. As a result, its rabbinical organizations have embraced these rabbis as members. The Conservative movement (through its United Synagogue of Conservative Judaism, the Jewish Theological Seminary of America, and the University of Judaism) is continuing to explore the issues of homosexuality.

Key words and phrases:

B'nai Noach: All the descendants of Noah who survived the flood along with his closet kin

If you want to know more:

Encyclopaedia Judaica. Jerusalem: Keter Publishing Co., 1975, 2:1189 ff.

Aaron Lichtenstein, *The Seven Laws of Noah.* New York and Brooklyn: Rabbi Jacob Joseph School Press and Z. Berman Books, 1981.

Psalm 31: Woman of Valor

The source:

Proverbs 31:10–31.

What you need to know:

1. It is traditional for a husband to read this section of Proverbs in honor of his spouse. This selection from Proverbs has become known as the "woman of valor" because of its descriptive opening phrase. It is read on Friday evening at the Sabbath dinner table before *kiddush* is recited. The passage describes the ideal wife.

2. Since the text is available in any volume of Hebrew Scriptures, here is an alternative translation by Rabbi Susan Grossman:

   A good wife, who can find her?
   She is worth far more than rubies.
   she brings good and not harm
   all the days of her life.
   She girds herself with strength
   and find her trades profitable.

   Wise counsel is on her tongue
   and her home never suffers for warmth.
   She stretches her hands to the poor,
   reaches her arms to the needy.
   All her friends praise her.
   Her family blesses her.
   She is known at the gates
   as she sits with the elders.
   Dignity, honor are her garb.
   She smiles at the future.

3. Some spouses choose to read a selection to honor their husbands. This translation takes the same text from Proverbs and modifies it for use by a woman for her husband. It is also by Rabbi Susan Grossman:

A good man, who can find him?
He is worth far more than rubies.
All who trust in him
never lack for gain.
He shares the household duties
and sets a goodly example.
He seeks a satisfying job
and braces his arms for work.
He opens his mouth with wisdom.
He speaks with love and kindness.
His justice brings him praises.
He raises the poor, lowers the haughty.

Sometimes, their children are invited to add:

These two indeed do worthily.
True leaders in Zion.
Give them their due credit.
Let their works praise them at the gates.

Things to remember

While it is traditional for a husband to read the text from Proverbs in honor of his wife, and the wife responds in many household in a like-mannered fashion, and children are blessed by their parents, there is no traditional provision for children to say anything in honor of their parents. Thus, children may want to write something and read it aloud at the Sabbath dinner table.

Key words and phrases

Eishet Chayil: Woman of valor

If you want to know more:

Ronald Isaacs, *Every Person's Guide to Shabbat*. Northvale, NJ: Jason Aronson, 1998.

Source:

Rabbi Yossi, son of Rabbi Judah said: "Two ministering angels accompany an individual on the eve of the Sabbath from the synagogue to home. One is a good angel and one is an evil one. And when the individual arrives home and finds the lamp burning, the table set, and the couch covered with a spread, the good angel exclaims, 'May it be even thus on another Sabbath too,' and the evil angel unwillingly responds 'Amen'. But if not [if the house is not prepared for Shabbat], the evil angel exclaims, 'May it be even thus on another Sabbath too,' and the good angel unwillingly responds 'Amen'."

Based on the Babylonian Talmud, *Shabbat* 119b.

What you need to know:

1. *Shalom Aleikhem* is a traditional hymn chanted on Friday nights, upon returning home from the Sabbath eve services. However, some synagogues sing it at the beginning of late Friday evening services (particularly in the Reform movement). Others sing it after services, before *kiddush*, in the synagogue, when late services are held.

2. This song of peace was said to be introduced by the kabbalists four centuries ago. It invites Sabbath angels to accompany the individual at the onset of Shabbat and stay with that person throughout Shabbat and then depart in peace at its conclusion.

שָׁלוֹם עֲלֵיכֶם מַלְאֲכֵי הַשָּׁרֵת מַלְאֲכֵי עֶלְיוֹן,
מִמֶּלֶךְ מַלְכֵי הַמְּלָכִים הַקָּדוֹשׁ בָּרוּךְ הוּא.

Shalom aleikhem malakhei ha-sharet malakhei elyon
Mi-melekh malkhei ha-mlakhim ha-kadosh barukh hu.

Peace be unto you, ministering angels, angels of the
  most High,
The Ruler of Rulers, the Holy Blessed One.

בּוֹאֲכֶם לְשָׁלוֹם מַלְאֲכֵי הַשָּׁלוֹם מַלְאֲכֵי עֶלְיוֹן,
מִמֶּלֶךְ מַלְכֵי הַמְּלָכִים הַקָּדוֹשׁ בָּרוּךְ הוּא.

Bo'akhem le-shalom malakhei ha-shalom malakhei elyon,
Mi-melekh malkhei ha-mlakhim ha-kadosh barukh hu.

Enter in peace, angels of peace, angels of the most
  High,
The Ruler of Rulers, the Holy Blessed One.

בָּרְכוּנִי לְשָׁלוֹם מַלְאֲכֵי הַשָּׁלוֹם מַלְאֲכֵי עֶלְיוֹן,
מִמֶּלֶךְ מַלְכֵי הַמְּלָכִים הַקָּדוֹשׁ בָּרוּךְ הוּא.

Barkhuni le-shalom malakhei ha-shalom malakhei elyon,
Mi-melekh malkhei ha-mlakhim ha-kadosh barukh hu.

Bless me with peace, angels of peace, angels of the
  most High.
The Ruler of Rulers, the Holy Blessed One.

צֵאתְכֶם לְשָׁלוֹם מַלְאֲכֵי הַשָּׁלוֹם מַלְאֲכֵי עֶלְיוֹן,
מִמֶּלֶךְ מַלְכֵי הַמְּלָכִים הַקָּדוֹשׁ בָּרוּךְ הוּא.

Tzetkhem le-shalom malakhei ha-shalom malakhei elyon,
Mi-melekh malkhei ha-mlakhim ha-kadosh barukh hu.

Depart in peace, angels of peace, angels of the most
  High,
The Ruler of Rulers, the Holy Blessed One.

Things to remember:

In many communities and in many families, individuals
either hold hands or embrace one another's shoulders
while singing *Shalom Aleikhem* and swaying back and forth.
This adds to the special time of the Sabbath.

Key words and phrases:

Malakhei Ha-sharet: Ministering angels
Shalom Aleikhem: Welcome

If you want to know more:

Encyclopaedia Judaica. Jerusalem: Keter Publishing House, 1975, 14:1286.

Instant Information
Jewish Ethical Advice

The source:

Various biblical and rabbinic sources, including Leviticus 19:18, Micah 6:8, Jeremiah 9:22–23, Psalm 15:1–5, Isaiah 33:15–16, Babylonian Talmud, *Makkot* 23b–24a, *Shabbat* 31a; Mishneh Peah 1:1.

What you need to know:

1. Ethics is part of the essence of Judaism. While the Reform movement describes Judaism as ethical monotheism, traditional Judaism argues that one of God's first concerns is with a person's decency. According to the Talmud, "In the hour when a person is brought before the heavenly court for judgment, one will be asked: 'Did you conduct your business affairs honestly? Did you set aside regular time for study? Did you try to have children? Did you look forward to the world's redemption?'"

2. Judaism teaches that it is through Torah study that a person learns to be a moral and ethical person. In addition, Jews have the obligation to perfect the world.

3. Here are some guiding principles culled from the Bible:

    i. God has told you what is good, and what is required of you:
    Do justly, love goodness and walk humbly with your God. (Micah 6:8)

    ii. Thus said God: Let not the wise person glory in one's wisdom, nor the strong one glory in one's strength. Let not the rich person glory in one's riches. Only in this should one glory: In one's earnest devotion to Me. For I God act with kindness, justice and equity in the world, and in these do I delight. (Jeremiah 9:22–23)

    iii. Love your neighbor as yourself. (Leviticus 19:18)

iv. God, who may sojourn in Your tent, and who may dwell in Your holy mountain? One who lives without blame, does right, and in one's heart acknowledges the truth. One whose tongue is not given to evil, who has never done harm to one's fellow human being or borne reproach for one's acts toward one's neighbor. For whom a contemptible person is abhorrent, but who honors those who fear God, who stands by one's oath even to one's own harm, who has never lent money at interest or accepted a bribe against the innocent. (Psalm 15:1–5)

v. One [is ethical] who walks in righteousness, speaks uprightly, spurns profit from fraudulent dealings, who waves away a bribe instead of taking it, who closes one's ears and does not listen to malicious words, who shuts one's eyes against looking at evil. (Isaiah 33:15–16)

4. Here are some guiding principles culled from rabbinic literature:

i. When Habakkuk came, he summed up the 613 commandments in one principle, for he said, "The righteous shall live according to his faith [2:4]." (Babylonian Talmud, *Makkot* 23b–24a)

ii. The world endures because of three things: Torah study, worship of God and deeds of kindness. (*Pirke Avot* 1:2)

iii. What is hateful to you, do not do to your neighbor. (Babylonian Talmud, *Shabbat* 31a)

Things to remember

According to the medieval philosopher/theologian Moses Maimonides, the purpose of the laws of the Torah is to bring mercy, lovingkindness and peace into the world. (*Mishneh Torah,* Laws of Shabbat, 2:3)

Key words and phrases:

Tikkun Olam: Perfection of the world
Ve'ahavta le'ray'ekha kamokha: Love your neighbor as yourself

If you want to know more:

Ronald Isaacs, *Derech Eretz: The Path to an Ethical Life*. New York: United Synagogue of Conservative Judaism, Department of Youth Activities, 1998.

Instant Information
Redeeming Captives

The source:

Babylonian Talmud, *Horayot* 13a; *Bava Batra* 8a–8b.

What you need to know:

1. It is a *mitzvah* to redeem captives and ransom Jews who are being held hostage. It is one of only a few commandments that deal with matters of life and death.

2. When several people are held hostage, Jewish law requires that women are to be ransomed first, because it is assumed that they will suffer greater abuse in captivity.

3. According to the rabbis, if a man and his father and his teacher are incarcerated, and the man only has enough money to redeem one person, then he (i.e., the man) takes precedence over his teacher in procuring ransom, while his teacher takes precedence over his father. He must procure the ransom of his teacher before that of his father. But his mother takes precedence over them all. A scholar takes precedence over a king, for if a scholar dies there is none to replace him, while all are eligible for kingship. (Babylonian Talmud, *Horayot* 13a)

4. Captives were not to be ransomed for more than their value, as a precaution for the general good. (Babylonian Talmud, *Gittin* 4:6)

5. According to Maimonides, there is no greater *mitzvah* than redemption of captives, for the problems of the captive include the problems of the hungry, the naked and those in mortal danger.

6. In recent years oppressed Jews of the Soviet Union, Ethiopia and Syria required the attention of the Jewish community. Thankfully many of them have

been successfully redeemed. But there is still more work to do, for even after they have been redeemed, they have to be absorbed into the community.

Things to remember:

1. In the 17th century, the Jewish community of Venice organized its own society for the redemption of captives (*chevrat pidyon shevuyim*) for the liberation of Jews incarcerated by pirates. Many other communities, from their example, appointed communal wardens to collect funds for the purpose of ransoming captives.

Key words and phrases:

Pidyon Shevuyim: Redeeming of captives

If you want to know more:

Barbara Fortgang Summers. *Community and Responsibility in Jewish Tradition*. New York: United Synagogue of America, Department of Youth Activities, 1978.

The Biblical Precepts Relevant to the Founding of the United States

Source:

Various Bible passages, including: Leviticus 25:10; Deuteronomy 16:20; Micah 6:8; Amos 5:26; Malachi 2:10; Psalm 133:1; and Proverbs 14:34.

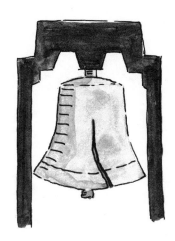

What you need to know:

Many American founding documents are clearly related to biblical precepts. Following is a listing of some of the more famous ones, along with their biblical counterparts.

1. "We hold these truths to be self-evident, that all men are created equal, that they are endowed by their Creator with certain inalienable rights, that among these are life, liberty and the pursuit of happiness" (Declaration of Independence).

   "Have we not all one Parent? Has not one God created us? Why should we be faithless to each other, profaning the covenant of our ancestors" (Malachi 2:10).

2. "We, the people of the United States, in order to form a more perfect union, establish justice, insure domestic tranquility, provide for the common defense, promote the general welfare, and secure the blessings of liberty to ourselves and our posterity, do ordain and establish a Constitution for the United States of America" (United States Constitution).

   "Justice, justice, shall you pursue, that you may thrive in the land which the Lord your God gives you" (Deuteronomy 16:20).

3. "Congress shall make no law respecting an establishment of religion, or prohibiting the free exercise thereof; or abridging the freedom of speech, or of the press; or of the right of the people to assemble, and to

petition the government for a redress of grievances" (The Bill of Rights).

"Proclaim liberty throughout the land, for all of its inhabitants" (Leviticus 25:10).

4. "Of all the dispositions and habits which lead to political prosperity, religion and morality are indispensable supports. Where is the security for property, for reputation, for life, if the sense of religious obligation desert the oaths which are the instruments of investigation in courts of justice? And let us with caution indulge the supposition that morality can be maintained without religion" (George Washington, Farewell Address).

"It has been told to you what is good, and what God requires of you: to act justly, to love mercy and to walk humbly with your God" (Micah 6:8).

5. "For happily the government of the United States which gives to bigotry no sanction, to persecution no assistance, requires only that they who live under its protection should demean themselves as good citizens in giving it on all occasions their effectual support" (George Washington, Letter to Newport Synagogue).

"Righteousness raises a nation to honor, but sin is disgraceful for any people" (Proverbs 14:34).

6. "We here highly resolve that these dead shall not have died in vain, that this nation, under God, shall have a new birth of freedom, and that government of the people, by the people, and for the people, shall not perish from the earth" (Abraham Lincoln, Gettysburg Address).

"How good and how pleasant it is when brothers [and sisters] live together in unity" (Psalm 133:1).

7. "With malice toward none, with charity for all, with firmness in the right as God gives us to see the right, let us strive to finish the work we are in . . . to do all which may achieve and cherish a just and lasting peace among ourselves, and with all nations" (Abraham Lincoln, Second Inaugural Address).

"Let justice roll on like a mighty river, righteousness like a never-ending stream" (Amos 5:26).

93

Things to remember:

There are many Bible phrases that continue to be used in everyday speech. Here are some examples:

1. "I have escaped with the **skin of my teeth**" (Job 19:20)

2. "**Am I my brother's keeper?**" (Genesis 4:9)

3. "Those who **spare the rod spoil the child**" (Proverbs 13:24)

4. "A person has no better thing under the sun, than to **eat, drink, and be merry**" (Ecclesiastes 8:15)

5. "I am **holier than thou**" (Isaiah 65:5)

6. "**Man does not live by bread alone**" (Deuteronomy 8:3)

7. "**Pride goes before a fall**" (Proverbs 16:18)

8. "**There is nothing new under** the sun" (Ecclesiastes 1:9)

Key words and phrases:

Tzedek, tzedek teerdof: Justice, justice you shall pursue

If you want to know more:

Ronald H. Isaacs. *The Jewish Bible Almanac*. Northvale, NJ: Jason Aronson, 1981.

Instant Information
Who's Who in Bible Commentators

Source:

Most of the classical commentators can be found in what is called *The Rabbis' Bible*: *Mikraot Gedolot*. Others are found in various sacred texts.

What you need to know:

Over the centuries numerous people have added their personal commentary to the Bible. Following is a partial listing of some of these commentators.

Ancient

Mekhilta: Oldest rabbinic commentary on Exodus (3rd century C.E.)

Midrash: Ancient sermonic explanations of the Torah and the Five Scrolls (1st through 10th century C.E.)

Philo Judaeus: Renowned Jewish philosopher in Alexandria, author of symbolic (allegorical) commentaries on the Five Books of Moses (2 B.C.E.–40 C.E.)

Septuagint: Greek translation of the Bible made by the Jews in Egypt (3rd century B.C.E.)

Sifra: Oldest rabbinic commentary on Leviticus

Sifre: Oldest rabbinic commentary on Numbers and Deuteronomy (4th century C.E.)

Medieval

Abraham ibn Ezra: Spanish biblical commentator (1092–1167)

Chizkuni: French commentator (13th century)

David Kimchi: French-Spanish biblical scholar (1160–1235)

Moses ben Nachman: Called the Ramban, a leading Spanish commentator (1194–1270)

Don Isaac Abarbanel: Spanish Bible commentator (1437–1509)

Joseph Bechor Shor: French commentator (12th century)

Obadiah Sforno. Italian commentator (1475–1550)

Rashi: Considered one of the greatest of all Bible commentators, this French Bible scholar was known for his literal interpretation of the Bible (1040–1105)

Modern

Israel Abrahams. Anglo-Jewish commentator (1858–1925)

David Altshul. Wrote popular commentaries on prophetic books (17th century)

Umberto Cassuto. Italian-Jewish commentator (1883–1951)

Samson Raphael Hirsch. German commentator (1808–1888)

Marcus Jastrow. American Bible scholar (1829–1903)

S. D. Luzzatto. Italian Hebraist and commentator (1800–1865)

Nehama Leibowitz. A Bible professor and commentator at the Hebrew University of Judaism

Malbim: Russian commentator (1809–1879)

Leopold Zunz: Edited and translated the Bible that is most used among German-speaking Jews (1794–1886)

Things to remember:

Various commentators were known to specialize in a particular style of explanation. The early rabbis compared the Torah to a beautiful garden whose fruits might be extracted by using four different methods signified by the Hebrew letters for the word for "orchard" or "paradise" *PaRDeS*:

P=Peshat: Commentator is interested in the literal interpretation of the Bible text (i.e., what the Bible meant to say at the time in which the passage was written). The commentator Rashi was master of the *Peshat* methodology.

R=Remez: The allegorical interpretation of the Bible, used by Philo, which hinted at information.

D=Derash: The sermonic, interpretative style, leading to the path of ethical and aggadic (stories, fables, legends) commentary.

S=Sod: The secretive and mystical interpretation of the Bible text, often used by students of the Kabbalah.

Key words and phrases:

Parshanut: Field of literature made up of commentaries and commentators.

If you want to know more:

Encyclopaedia Judaica. Jerusalem: Keter Publishing Co., 1975, 4:890–892.
Joseph Hertz, ed., *The Pentateuch and Haftorahs.* London: Soncino Press, 1987.

The source:

Various Talmudic sources, including these tractates of the Babylonian Talmud: *Pesachim* and *Horayot*, *Gittin* and *Shabbat*.

What you need to know:

Much of ancient medicine consisted of a combination of science, superstition and folklore. As we explore "alternative" or "complementary" forms of medicine in the postmodern world, the challenge remains as to how to determine one from the other! Supernatural agencies were often considered as causes of illness and disease, and remedies often included incantations accompanied by other rites and rituals. Following are several rabbinic passages which reflect the many recipes that belong to the category of folk medicine.

1. **Remedy for an intermittent fever:** Rabbi Huna said: As a remedy for a fever, one should procure seven prickles from seven date palms, seven chips from seven beams, seven pegs from seven bridges, seven handfuls of ash from seven ovens, seven pinches of earth from seven graves, seven bits of pitch from seven ships, seven seeds of cumin, and seven hairs from the beard of an old dog, and tie them inside the collar of his shirt with a band of twined strands of wool. (Babylonia Talmud, *Shabbat* 67a)

2. **Remedy for depression:** If a person is seized by depression, eat red meat broiled over coals and drink diluted wine. (Babylonian Talmud, *Gittin* 67b)

3. **Remedy for a migraine headache**: For a migraine, one should take a woodcock and cut its throat with a white silver coin over the side of the head where the pain is concentrated, taking care that the blood does not blind the eyes. Then hang the bird on the doorpost, so that

the person can rub against it when coming in and when exiting. (Babylonia Talmud, *Gittin* 69a)

4. **Remedy for cataracts:** Take a seven-hued scorpion, dry it out in the shade, and mix two parts of ground kohl to one part of ground scorpion. Then, with a paintbrush, apply three drops to each eye—no more, lest the eye burst. (Babylonian Talmud, *Gittin* 69a)

5. **Remedy to stop a nosebleed**: Call a priest whose name is Levi and write "Levi" backward, or else call any other man and write backward, "I am Papa Shila bar Sumki," or else write "the taste of the bucket in water of blemish." (Babylonian Talmud, *Gittin* 69a)

6. **Remedy for a toothache:** For a toothache, Rabbah bar R. Chuna said: Take a whole head of garlic, grind it with oil and salt and apply it on his thumbnail to the side where the tooth aches. Put a rim of dough around it, thus taking care that it does not touch the flesh, as it may cause leprosy. (Babylonian Talmud, *Gittin* 69a)

7. **Remedy for heartburn:** Take black cumin regularly. (Babylonian Talmud, *Berakhot* 40a)

8. **Remedy for bad breath:** After every food eat salt, and after every beverage drink water and you will come to no harm. (Babylonian Talmud, *Berakhot* 40a)

Things to remember:

Because of the importance of medicine and the treatment of the body, the Babylonian Talmud (*Sanhedrin* 17b) enumerates ten things that must be in a city where a scholar lives. Among these requirements are a physician and a surgeon.

Key words and phrases:

Rofeh: doctor

If you want to know more:

Ronald H. Isaacs, *Judaism, Medicine and Healing*. Northvale, NJ: Jason Aronson, 1998.

Prophets of the Bible

The source:

Rashi's commentary on the Talmud lists the prophets (Babylonian Talmud, *Megillah* 14), as do the collections of *Halakhot Gedolot* and *Seder Olam*. Some of the information in this section can be culled directly from a reading of the Bible itself.

What you need to know:

1. The Hebrew word for "prophet," *navi*, signifies a spokesperson, one who speaks for God to human beings.

2. Foreseeing the outcome of national crises and evil practices, the prophets fearlessly criticized the morals of their own day while teaching a nobler way of living.

3. The message of the prophets was usually one of warning and exhortation, including a prediction of coming events in the near or distant future.

4. While we may not normally have called some of the following individuals prophets, according to the medieval commentator Rashi, these are the forty-eight male prophets and seven female prophets:

Male Prophets

1. **Abraham**: (18th century B.C.E.) The son of Terach and a descendant of Eber, Abraham was the father of the Israelite nation and the first to preach monotheism to the world.

2. **Aaron**: (13th century B.C.E.) Brother of Moses, served as intermediary between Moses and Pharaoh because of his eloquence.

3. **Ahijah the Shilonite**: (10th century B.C.E.) Active toward the end of Solomon's reign, speaking in God's

name, he prophesied the division of the kingdom "because they have forsaken Me and they have not walked in My ways, to do that which is right in my eyes, and to keep My statutes and My ordinances, as did David" (I Kings 11:33).

4. **Amos**: (8th century B.C.E.) Native of Tekoa, this minor prophet prophesied in the days of Uzziah, Jeroboam II, Jotham, Ahaz, and Hezekiah. He was the first prophet whose utterances have been transmitted to us in a separate book.

5. **Amoz**: (8th century B.C.E.) According to the sages, he was the brother of King Amaziah. He opposed the importing of troops from the Northern Kingdom to aid Judah (II Chronicles 25:15–16).

6. **Azariah, son of Oded**: (8th century B.C.E.) During the reign of Asa, King of Judah, Azariah prophesied: "God is with you, while you are with God. Be strong, and let not your hands be slack, for your work shall be rewarded" (II Chronicles 15:1–2, 7). Asa eventually removed the detestable idols from the land of Judah and Benjamin.

7. **Baruch, son of Neriah**: (6th century B.C.E.) Scribe and student of Jeremiah, Baruch "wrote from the mouth of Jeremiah all the words of God, which God has spoken to him, upon a roll of a book" (Jeremiah 36:4).

8. **Chaggai**: (10th century B.C.E.) This post-exilic prophet, whose book is the tenth of the minor prophets, called for rebuilding of the Temple.

9. **Chanani the Seer**: (5th century B.C.E.) He rebuked Asa, king of Judah, for relying on the king of Aram when in danger, and not upon God (II Chronicles 16).

10. **David**: (10th century B.C.E.) The rabbinic sages observed that David, too, was a prophet, because the Bible says, "to whom David and Samuel the seer did ordain in their office" (I Chronicles 9:22).

11. **Eli the Priest**: (11th century B.C.E.) He was the predecessor of Samuel, the last of the judges, and was the last High Priest in the Tabernacle of Shiloh.

Eli was revered by all, and his blessing was prized as one that came from the lips of the holy man of God (I Samuel 1:17).

12. **Eliezer, son of Dodavahu**: (9th century B.C.E.) A Judean prophet, Eliezer told Jehoshaphat, "Because you have joined yourself with Ahaziah, God has made a breach in your works." Jehoshaphat, refusing to heed the prophet's words, made an agreement with the king of Israel to have ships built in Ezion-geber. However, before the vessels were able to sail for Tarshish, their destination, they were destroyed (II Chronicles 20:35–37)

13. **Elijah**: (9th century B.C.E.) Native of Gilead, he prophesied and brought miracles in the kingdom of Ephraim during the reigns of Ahab and his son Ahaziah. He waged an endless struggle against Jezebel and the Baal cult which she had brought to Israel from her birthplace (I Kings 19:1–21). Because of his ascent to heaven while still alive, Jewish tradition holds that he will announce the arrival of the Messiah.

14. **Elisha:** (9th century B.C.E.) Son of Shaphat, he was the disciple and successor of Elijah. He had an extraordinary career, performing even more miracles than did Elijah. For instance, he purified the fountain in Jericho (II Kings 2:19–22) and miraculously increased a widow's supply of oil (II Kings 4:1–7).

15. **Elkanah:** (11th century B.C.E.) Son of Jeroham, a family of the tribe of Levi (I Chronicles 6:19–24). According to rabbinic tradition (Babylonian Talmud *Megillah* 14), he was one of the major prophets, unparalleled in his generation.

16. **Ezekiel:** (6th century B.C.E.) Third of the three major prophets, he witnessed the destruction of Jerusalem and Judea and went into exile to Babylonia. Chapter 37 of his book describes his famous vision of the valley of dry bones that are resurrected, symbolizing the rebirth of Israel.

17. **Gad the Seer:** (10th century B.C.E.) The Bible refers to Gad as both prophet and seer (I Chronicles 29:29).

102

He helped David to organize the Levitical singers in the Temple (I Chronicles 23:27).

18. **Habakkuk**: (7th century B.C.E.) His book is the eighth of the minor prophets. It is an outcry against the victory of the Chaldeans and the rule of iniquity in the world.

19. **Hosea**: (8th century B.C.E.) He was the first man whose own failed marriage symbolized Israel's relationship with God. His book is considered to be one of the minor prophetic books.

20. **Iddo the Seer**: (10th century B.C.E.) According to the sages, Iddo preached during the reign of Jeroboam, son of Nebat. It was he who came from Judah to Bethel and prophesied the destruction of the altar that Jeroboam had built there and had sacrificed upon.

21. **Isaac**: (17th century B.C.E.) Only son of Abraham by his wife Sarah, Isaac was the second of the patriarchs.

22. **Isaiah**: (8th century B.C.E.) He prophesied from the year of Uzziah's death until the beginning of Manasseh's reign. He is considered one of the three major classical prophets.

23. **Jacob**: (16th century B.C.E.) Son of Isaac, Jacob was the third of the patriarchs and father of the twelve tribes of Israel.

24. **Jehu son of Chanani**: (9th century B.C.E.) Prophesying during the reign of Asa, he declared that Baasa, ruler of the Northern Kingdom, would suffer Jeroboam's fate. Jehu also wrote the chronicles of Jehoshaphat (II Chronicles 20:34).

25. **Jeremiah**: (7th century B.C.E.) This major prophet with his own book belonged to a priestly family in Anatot near Jerusalem. His prophecies foretold the doom of his people as punishment for their sins.

26. **Joel**: (5th century B.C.E.) Second in the order of the twelve minor prophets, Joel called the people of Judea to repent because the Day of Judgment was at hand.

27. **Jonah, son of Amittai**: (8th century B.C.E.) According to the book that bears his name, Jonah was sent to

Nineveh to make the people repent of their evil doing. He fled the country, only to be swallowed by a large fish. In the end he was forced to come to Nineveh, and there successfully encouraged its inhabitants to repent.

28. **Joshua**: (13th century B.C.E.) Son of Nun, Joshua belonged to the tribe of Ephraim. He led the Israelites in battle in the desert against Amalek whom he defeated in Rephidim. (Exodus 17:8) He succeeded Moses and conquered the seven nations of Canaan.

29. **Machseiah**: (7th century B.C.E.) He was the father of Neriah and grandfather of Baruch, the scribe of Jeremiah (Jeremiah 32:12).

30. **Malachi**: (5th century B.C.E.) Last of the biblical prophets, he protests against transgressions in matters of sacrifices and tithes and complains of mixed and broken marriages.

31. **Micah**: (12th century B.C.E.) This minor prophet spoke out against the social evils of his time, maintaining that they would bring about the nation's downfall.

32. **Micaiah, son of Imlah**: (9th century B.C.E.) In the days of Ahab, Micaiah was the only true prophet among some 400 court prophets who told the king whatever he wanted to hear (I Kings 22:8). According to the Bible, he beheld God and the heavenly angels: "I saw God sitting on the throne, and all the heavenly host standing by God on the right hand and on the left" (I Kings 22:19).

33. **Mordecai**: (5th century B.C.E.) A descendant of Kish, he lived in Shushan and reared Esther, his cousin. With her help, he was able to thwart the evil Haman's schemes and bring retribution upon the enemies of Israel.

34. **Moses**: (13th century B.C.E.) Considered the greatest of the prophets. Of him the Bible says: "There has not arisen a prophet since in Israel like Moses, whom God knew face to face" (Deuteronomy 34:10). Moses had a strong influence on all the prophets who followed him. The Jewish people received the Torah through Moses at Sinai.

35. **Nahum**: (7th century B.C.E.) He lived during the reign of Manasseh and foretold the fall of Nineveh.

36. **Nathan the Prophet**: (10th century B.C.E.) Nathan was a prophet in the generation that followed Samuel. He admonished David fearlessly for the latter's misconduct with Bathsheba (II Samuel 12:13 ff.).

37. **Neriah**: (7th century B.C.E.) He was the father of Baruh and one of the eight prophets descended from Rahab, a woman of Jericho (Jeremiah 36:4).

38. **Obadiah**: (5th century B.C.E.) He was the fourth of the so-called minor prophets. In his one-chapter book, he predicts the destruction of Edom and condemns the Edomites for having refused to assist Jerusalem in the days of calamity.

39. **Oded**: (10th century B.C.E.) Oded prophesied in Samaria during the reign of Ahaz, king of Judah, and Pekah, son of Remaliah, king of Israel.

40. **Pinchas**: (11th century B.C.E.) Grandson of Aaron, in reward for his zealous action against Zimri, he and his descendants were promised the priesthood (Numbers 25).

41. **Samuel**: (11th century B.C.E.) Son of Elkanah and the last judge of Israel. As an adult he attained fame as a prophet throughout the land.

42. **Seraiah, son of Neriah**: (6th century B.C.E.) According to the sages, he prophesied during the second year of Darius' reign. He appears in the fifty-first chapter of the Book of Jeremiah.

43. **Shemaiah**: (10th century B.C.E.) A Judean, Shemaiah prophesied during the reign of Rehoboam when the latter mustered his army in hopes of regaining his sovereignty over the Northern Kingdom.

44. **Solomon**: (10th century B.C.E.) The rabbinic sages included King Solomon among the prophets because of his dream at Gibeon. God appeared to him there and said, "Ask what I shall give you." Solomon requested "an understanding heart" to judge the people (I Kings 3:5, 9).

45. **Uriah, son of Shemaiah**: (6th century B.C.E.) Native of Kiriath-jearim, Uriah prophesied during the reign of Jehoiakim. He foretold the destruction of the city and the country in much the same way as did Jeremiah.

46. **Yechaziel the Levite**: (10th century B.C.E.) In II Chronicles 20:14, we learn that "the spirit of God came upon Yechaziel." He encouraged Jehoshaphat prior to the battle against Ammon, Moab and Seir.

47. **Zechariah**: (6th century B.C.E.) This minor prophet's prophecies are concerned with contemporary events and foretell the ingathering of the exiles and the expansion of Jerusalem.

48. **Zephaniah**: (7th century B.C.E.) The prophecies of this minor prophet were mostly eschatological. Described in his book is the Day of the Lord, when God will punish all the wicked and God will be universally acknowledged.

Female Prophets

1. **Abigail**: (10th century B.C.E.) The Bible records that Abigail prophesied to David: "God will certainly make my lord a sure house" (I Samuel 25:28–31).

2. **Channah**: (11th century B.C.E.) She was the mother of the prophet Samuel.

3. **Chuldah:** (7th century B.C.E.) The wife of Shallu, she lived near the courts of learning in Jerusalem during the reign of Josiah (II Kings 22:14). The sages (Babylonian Talmud, *Megillah* 14b) declared that Chuldah was one of the three prophets of that generation; the other two were Zephaniah and Jeremiah.

4. **Deborah**: (12th century B.C.E.) The Bible refers to Deborah as "a prophet, the wife of Lapidot." She fought a famous battle against Sisera and successfully defeated his army (Judges 4).

5. **Esther**: (5th century B.C.E.) The rabbis regarded Esther as a prophet because the Bible says of her: "Esther put on her royal apparel" (Esther 5:1) This

was interpreted to mean that she was clothed with the divine spirit, as it is similarly written: "The spirit clothed Amasai" (I Chronicles 12:19; cf. Babylonian Talmud, *Megillah* 4b).

6. **Miriam**: (13th century B.C.E.) The Bible explicitly refers to Miriam as a prophet: "And Miriam the prophet took the timbrel" (Exodus 15:20). She was the sister of Moses, considered the greatest prophet to have ever lived.

7. **Sarah**: (18th century B.C.E.) Sarah, the wife of Abraham, bore Isaac. Today she is considered one of the four Jewish matriarchs.

Things to remember:

1. The literary prophets were so called because their words were written down in books that were named for them.

2. Many of the prophets preached the importance of being ethical and moral.

3. The fundamental experience of the prophet is a fellowship with God.

Key words and phrases:

Navi: prophet

If you want to know more:

Ronald Isaacs, *Messengers of God: A Jewish Prophets Who's Who*. Northvale, NJ: Jason Aronson, 1998.

The source:

A cross-section of some of the names of God, culled from the Bible, the prayer book, and various rabbinic sources.

What you need to know:

1. Jewish tradition says that the name of God, which consists of the four Hebrew letters *yod, heh, vav, heh,* was revealed to Moses at the burning bush. Its exact pronunciation was passed on to his brother Aaron and kept a secret among the priests.

2. The only time when the High Priest actually pronounced the name of God was on Yom Kippur (Day of Atonement), during the confession of sins.

3. When people were not in the ancient sanctuary, the euphemism *Adonai* was used as the name for God.

4. In conversation, the term *HaShem* ("The Name") is often used to protect God's name from possible blasphemy and improper use, particularly among traditional Jews.

God in the Bible

1. *El:* The oldest Semitic term for God, it is a descriptive name, often used in combination with other names for God. For example, *El Olam* (Eternal God) or *El Shaddai* (Almighty God).

2. *Elohim:* Appears in the opening verse of the Torah: "In the beginning, God (Elohim) created the heaven and the earth" (Genesis 1:1).

3. *YHVH* (alternatively *YHWH*): An ancient biblical name for God, possibly pronounced Yahweh. The consensus of scholarly opinion is that *YHVH* is derived from a form of the verb "to be."

4. *El Shaddai*: Divine Name frequently found in the Bible and often translated "Almighty."

5. *Adonai*: Derived from the Hebrew *Adon* (Lord).

6. *Yah*: A short form of the Divine Name (*Yh*), Yah may represent the original form from which YHVH was expanded. Yah also appears in biblical names such as Elijah (*Eliyahu* in Hebrew).

7. *Adonai Tzeva'ot*: "Lord of Hosts (i.e., God's angels) is the traditional translation of this Divine Name. Some say that it means "One who brings the angelic hosts into being."

8. *Kadosh*: The Holy One.

9. *Tzur*: The Rock.

10. *Ehyeh asher Ehyeh*: "I am that I am" (Exodus 3:14).

Rabbinic Names for God

1. *HaKadosh Barukh Hu*: The Holy Blessed One.

2. *Ribbono shel Olam*: Sovereign of the Universe.

3. *Hamakom*: The Place or the Omnipresent One.

4. *Avinu Shebashamayim*: Our Father in Heaven.

5. *Ein Sof*: Kabbalistic name, meaning "Without End."

6. *Shalom*: Peace.

7. *Temira detemirin*: Kabbalistic name, meaning "Hidden of Hiddens."

God's Names in the Prayerbook

1. *Elohay Avraham*: God of Abraham.

2. *Elohay Yitzchak*: God of Isaac.

3. *Elohay Ya'akov*: God of Jacob.

4. *Shomer Yisrael*: Guardian of Israel.

5. *Melekh Malkhai hamelakhim*: Sovereign of Sovereigns.

6. *Adon Olam*: Eternal God.

7. *Harofe*: The Healer.

8. *Tzur Yisrael*: Rock of Israel.

Things to remember:

1. The various names of God reflect descriptions of different aspects of God as our ancestors experienced the Divine.

2. The rabbis prescribed injunctions regarding the writing of God's name. For example, if the name of God is written, it cannot be erased. It can be discarded only through ritual burial, just like sacred texts.

Key words and phrases:

Chillul HaShem: Profaning of God's Name
Kiddush Hashem: Sanctification of God's Name

If you want to know more:

Steven Brown, *Higher and Higher: Making Jewish Prayer Part of Us*. New York: United Synagogue of America, Department of Youth Activities, 1985.

Ronald Isaacs, *Close Encounters: Jewish Views About God*. Northvale, NJ: Jason Aronson, 1996.

Instant Information
Jewish Numerology

The source:

The Bible and various rabbinic sources.

What you need to know:

1. The Jewish Bible is full of numbers. Some were to be taken literally, while others are symbols or metaphors.

2. With the advent of *gematria* (i.e., rabbinic numerology), rabbis began to use *gematria* to explain various Jewish texts.

3. A cross-section of interesting numbers from Jewish life:

   a. **Longest verse in the Bible**: Appears in the Book of Esther (8:9) which has 43 words in Hebrew.

   b. **Rabbinic teacher mentioned the most times**: Rabbi Yehuda bar Ilai is mentioned 607 times in the Mishnah.

   c. **The human life cycle**: This passage from *Pirke Avot* presents the ages of readiness for responsibilities in life.

   The age of 5 for the study of Bible.
   The age of 10 for the study of Mishnah.
   The age of 13 for being responsible for the commandments.
   The age of 15 for the study of Talmud.
   The age of 18 for marriage.
   The age of 20 for earning a living.
   The age of 30 for power.
   The age of 40 for understanding.
   The age of 50 for giving advice.
   The age of 60 for old age.
   The age of 70 for gray hairs.
   The age of 80 for special strength.
   The age of 90 for bowed back.

The age of 100—it is as if one had died and passed away.

d. **The number 7 as a rabbinic remedy for fever**: To cure a fever, take 7 prickles from 7 palm trees, 7 chips from 7 beams, 7 nails from 7 bridges, 7 ashes from 7 ovens, 7 scoops of earth from 7 door sockets, 7 pieces of pitch from 7 ships, 7 handfuls of cumin, and 7 hairs from the beard of an old dog, and tie them to the neck hole of the shirt with a twisted cord. (Babylonian Talmud, *Shevuot* 15b)

e. **The number 12 in Jewish life:** Following are the appearances of the number 12 in Jewish life:

12 tribes of Israel (Reuben, Simeon, Levi, Judah, Issachar, Zebulun, Joseph, Benjamin, Dan, Naphtali, Gad, and Asher)
12 stones in the breastplate of the High Priest
12 minor prophets: Hosea, Joel, Amos, Obadiah, Jonah, Micah, Nachum, Habakkuk, Zephaniah, Haggai, Zechariah, and Malachi
12 months in the year
12 constellations
Jewish girl is obligated to fulfill *mitzvot* at age 12
12 loaves of shewbread used in the tabernacle
12 portions in the Book of Genesis
At age 12 King Solomon became king.

f. **Bible Statistics:** The Bible has more than 773,000 words and 3.5 million letters. There are 39 books in the Jewish Bible, 929 chapters, and 23,214 verses.

g. **Number 70 in the writings of the Rabbis**:

i. Gog and Magog have the numerical value of 70, namely the 70 nations.

ii. The Torah was transmitted to the 70 elders. *(Midrash Yelamdeinu)*

iii. There are 70 facets to the Torah. (*Zohar Bereshit* 36)

iv. Seventy facets to the Torah were translated into 70 languages in order to make it more understandable to the 70 nations. (Babylonian Talmud, *Sotah* 32a)

v. On the Festival of Sukkot, 70 sacrifices were offered for the sake of the 70 nations of the world who have 70 representatives among the heavenly angels. *(Midrash Alpha Beita)*

If you want to know more:

Ronald Isaacs, *The Jewish Book of Numbers*. Northvale, NJ: Jason Aronson, 1996.

Jewish Superstitions

The source:

Various rabbinic sources, including the Talmud and other kabbalistic sources.

What you need to know:

1. Over time each community has developed its own particular folk customs and practices that are associated with it. Within the world of folklore one will usually find a variety of superstitions.

2. A superstition is generally defined as any custom or act that is based on an irrational fear rather than on tradition, belief, reason, or knowledge.

3. Many Jewish superstitions evolved with the goal of safeguarding a person from danger and evil.

4. A cross-section of Judaism's superstitions, many of which continue to play an important role in the life of a contemporary Jew:

   i. **Superstition related to circumcision:** Place red ribbons and garlic on a baby's crib to ward off evil spirits. Also, keep candy under the bed to draw attention of evil spirits away from baby.

   ii. **Superstition related to naming a child:** Some Jews have the custom of refusing to marry a person who has the same name as their mother or father. This custom arose from fear that the Angel of Death might confuse two persons with the same name, leading to the premature death of one or the other.

   iii. **Superstition and the wedding:** Brides often carried a lighted torch or candle as a way of warding off evil spirits. Also, the custom of the fast of a bride and groom on the day of their wedding is intended to fool the evil spirits into thinking that it is a day of mourning rather than one of ultimate joy.

114

iv. **Superstition and death**: Watching and caring for a deceased person (before burial) while reading various psalms was considered a strong antidote to evil spirits.

v. **Superstition and saliva:** Expectorating and using one's saliva was an ancient way of repelling evil spirits. Today, saying the phrase "pooh pooh pooh" after witnessing or acknowledging something wonderful or beautiful such as a newborn baby is considered an antidote to evil.

vi. **Superstition and books**: Closing books that are left open is a superstitious practice that likely relates to the ancient belief that an open book can be more easily inhabited by an evil spirit who can work to distort its meaning.

vii. **Superstition and the evil eye:** Put a piece of matzah into the pocket of a particularly handsome child to protect him or her against the evil eye. Qualify any praise that you give a beautiful object or person with the phrase *kein hore* (Yiddish for "no evil") or *kein ayen hore* (Yiddish for "no evil eye"), often shortened to *kaynahora*.

viii. **Superstition and counting people**: Never count people using one, two, three, etc., because numbering people creates a special susceptibility to the evil eye. If you need to count people, count "not one," "not two," and so on.

Key words and phrases:

Ayin Hara: Evil eye

If you want to know more:

Brenda Z. Rosenbaum and Stuart Copans, *How to Avoid the Evil Eye*. New York: St Martin's Press, 1985.

Joshua Trachtenberg, *Jewish Magic and Superstition: A Study in Folk Religion*. New York: Behrman House, 1939.

Notable Quotations from the Bible

The source:

The Jewish Bible, especially the Book of Proverbs.

What you need to know:

1. The Bible is filled with pithy sayings and proverbs, many of which have entered into contemporary conversation.

2. The fifteenth book of the Bible, called Proverbs, contains a plethora of sayings concerning industry, sobriety, honesty, caution and learning.

3. A cross-section of proverbs and notable sayings from various Bible sources:

   a. The fear of God is the beginning of knowledge. (Proverbs 1:7)
   b. The one who spares the rod spoils the child. (Proverbs 13:24)
   c. Go to the ant, you sluggard, consider her ways and be wise. (Proverbs 6:6)
   d. Hate stirs up strife, but love covers all transgressions. (Proverbs 10:2)
   e. A word fitly spoken is like apples of gold in settings of silver. (Proverbs 25:1)
   f. Am I my brother's keeper? (Genesis 4:9)
   g. Cast your bread upon the waters, for after many days you will find it. (Ecclesiastes 11:1)
   h. An eye for an eye, a tooth for a tooth. (Exodus 21:24)
   i. Not by might, nor by power, but by My spirit, says the Lord of Hosts. (Zechariah 4:6)
   j. The Lord is my shepherd and I shall not want. (Psalm 23:1)

If you want to know more:

A. Colin Day, *Roget's Thesaurus of the Bible*. San Francisco: Harper Collins, 1992.

Instant Information
Best Times to Get Married

The source:

Various rabbinic and talmudic sources.

What you need to know:

1. Weddings among traditional Jews are not performed:

   on Sabbaths and festivals; during the intermediate days of Passover and Sukkot;

   during periods of national mourning, such as the days of *sefirah* (counting the omer) between Passover and Shavuot and what are called the "three weeks" between the seventeenth of Tammuz and the Ninth of Av.

2. One should consult his or her own rabbi concerning days when weddings may take place, since there are also times when it is considered inconvenient for the community or inappropriate even if there is no Jewish law preventing it.

3. Certain days are considered lucky for wedding ceremonies. They include:

   a. Tuesdays, because in describing the third day of creation (i.e., Tuesday), the Bible twice uses the expression "God saw that this was good" (Genesis 1:10, 12).
   b. Wednesdays for virgins, and Thursday for widows
   c. Israel Independence Day, Lag B'Omer and Tu B'Av (the 15th day of Av)
   d. During the month of Elul, before the High Holidays. Elul is considered a month for love because the word Elul is an acronym formed from the Hebrew words in the Song of Songs, *Ani Le-dodi, Ve-dodi Li,* "I am my beloved's and my beloved is mine."

Key words and phrases:

Ani Le-dodi: I am my beloved's and my beloved is mine.

If you want to know more:

Maurice Lamm, *The Jewish Way in Love and Marriage*. San Francisco: Harper and Row, 1980.

Instant Information
The Confessional

The source:

"When a person is sick and near death, that person is required to make confession" (Babylonian Talmud, *Shabbat* 32a).

What you need to know:

1. Observant Jews make confession on their deathbed, in keeping with the talmudic instruction that one who is near death is asked to do so.

2. While there are a variety of texts that may be used for the confessional, here is one that is commonly used:

   My God and God of my ancestors, accept my prayer. Do not turn away. Forgive me for all the times I may have disappointed You. I am aware of the wrongs I have committed.

   May my pain and suffering serve as atonement. Forgive my shortcomings, for against You I have sinned.

   May it be Your will, Adonai my God and God of my ancestors, that I live now with a clear conscience and in accordance with Your will. Send a *refuah sheleimah*, a complete healing, to me and to all who suffer.

   My life and death are in Your hands, Adonai my God. May it be Your will to heal me.

   Guardian of the bereaved, protect my beloved family; our souls are bound together. In Your hands lies my spirit.

   Hear O Israel: Adonai is our God, Adonai is One.

   Adonai is God. Adonai is God.[1]

---

[1] Excerpted from the *Rabbis Manual*. New York: Rabbinical Assembly, 1998.

More Particulars

Since the only way to complete full *teshuva*, according to many authorities, is through one's death, even criminals are urged to confess within a short distance of the scene of their execution. If they have nothing to confess, they are instructed to say: "Let my death be an atonement for all of my transgressions" (Babylonian Talmud, *Sanhedrin* 6:2).

Key words and phrases:

Vidui: Confession

If you want to know more:

Simon Glustrom, *The Language of Judaism*. Northvale, NJ: Jason Aronson, 1966.

Instant Information
Sing *Hava Nagilah*

The source:

Lyrics composed by Cantor Moshe Nathanson (cantor of the Society for the Advancement of Judaism). Based on the verse from the Book of Psalms (118:24): *"Zeh hayom asah Adonai nagilah v'nismecha bo.* This is the day that God has made, let us be happy and rejoice on it."

What you need to know:

1. *Hava Nagilah* is probably the world's most famous Hebrew song of joy.

2. The melody for *Hava Nagilah* was composed by A. Z. Idelsohn, famous Jewish musicologist, who is often considered the founder of modern Jewish musicology

3. The text for *Hava Nagilah*, often accompanied by a dance (the *hora* circle dance):

הָבָה נָגִילָה

וְנִשְׂמְחָה

הָבָה נְרַנְּנָה

וְנִשְׂמְחָה

עוּרוּ עוּרוּ אַחִים

עוּרוּ אַחִים בְּלֵב שָׂמֵחַ

Hava Nagilah (3)
V'nismecha
Hava n'ranana (3)
V'nismecha
Uru uru achim
Uru achim b'lev sameach

Come, let us be joyful
And let our happiness overflow.
Come, let us rejoice

And let our happiness overflow.
Rise, rise, O brethren,
Rise, O brethren.

Things to remember:

The melody for *Hava Nagilah* was adapted from a hasidic tune. Few songfests, Jewish weddings, bar or bat mitzvah celebrations are considered complete without the singing of *Hava Nagilah*.

Key words and phrases:

Hava Nagilah: Come, let us be joyful

If you want to know more:

Sheldon Feinberg, *Hava Nagila: The World's Most Famous Song of Joy*. New York: Shapolsky Publishers, 1988.

Instant Information
Who's Who in Rabbinic Commentators

The source:

Various editions of the Talmud contain commentaries on the Talmud. Some include biographical information of sorts. Easier access for this information is provided in: Moses Mielziner, *Introduction to the Talmud*. New York: Bloch Publishing, 1925.

What you need to know:

1. A knowledge of the dates of the rabbinic commentators (known as Tannaim—the early teachers—and the Amoraim—the later teachers) and the chronological order of the generations in which they lived can be of help in understanding different aspects of Talmudic discussion.

2. Amoraim is the title given to Jewish scholars in Palestine and Babylonia in the 3rd through the 6th centuries C.E. The Amoraim continued the work of the Tannaim, teachers living during the first two centuries C.E. in Palestine.

3. The chronology of rabbinic scholars can help to demonstrate the evolution of opinions among the rabbis, as well as how they conflict and contrast with one another.

4. Many sages had identical names. Thus, it is often difficult to determine whether a statement should be ascribed to the first, second, or even third scholar bearing that name.

5. Following is a summary of the important rabbinic scholars during both the Tannaitic and Amoraic periods:

Tannaitic Period

Date	Tannaim	Historical Events in Israel
3rd cent. B.C.E.	Shimon HaTzaddik	Conquest of Israel by Alexander the Great
	Antigonos of Sokho	
2nd cent. B.C.E.	Yose ben Yoezer Yose ben Yochanan Nitai HaArbeli	Maccabees
1st cent. B.C.E.	Yehudah ben Tabbi Alexander Yannai Shimon ben Shetach Shemayah, Avtalyon	
30 B.C.E.– 20 B.C.E.	Hillel, Shammai	Herodian period
20 C.E.–40 C.E.	Gamliel HaZaken	Herodian period
40 C.E.–80 C.E.	Shimon ben Gamliel I	Second Temple destroyed
	Yochanan ben Zakkai	
80 C.E.–110 C.E.	Gamliel II of Yavneh Eliezer ben Hyrcanus	
110 C.E.–135 C.E.	Akiva	Bar Kokhba revolt
135 C.E.–170 C.E.	Shimon ben Gamliel II Shimon bar Yochai	
170 C.E.–200 C.E.	Yehudah HaNasi	Final redaction of Mishnah

Amoraic Period

Dates	Israel	Babylonia	World Events
200 C.E.–220 C.E.	Oshaya Rabbah Bar Kappara Hiyya		
220 C.E.–250 C.E.	Hanina ben Hama	Rav, Shmuel	Sassanid kingdom
250 C.E.–290 C.E.	Yochanan ben Nappacha Resh Lakish	Huna Yehudah	
290 C.E.–320 C.E.	Ammi, Assi, Zera	Rabbah, Yosef	Sassanid kingdom
320 C.E.–350 C.E.	Hillel II, Yonah, Yose	Abaye, Rava,	Christianity
350 C.E.–375 C.E.	Mana II Tanchuma bar Abba	Ashi, Ravina I	Jerusalem Talmud
	Mar ben Rav Ashi		
460 C.E.–500 C.E.	Rabbah Tosafa'ah Ravina II		Final redaction of Babylonian Talmud

Key words and phrases:

Amora (plural, *Amoraim*: Title given to Jewish scholars in Palestine and Babylonia in the 3rd–6th centuries.

Tanna (plural, *Tannaim*): Teacher mentioned in Mishnah (first two centuries C.E.)

If you want to know more:

Jacob Neusner, *Invitation to Talmud*. New York: Harper and Row, 1973.

The source:

The best source for this information is through the obser-vance and participation in Sephardic communities. However, it should be noted that customs differ depend-ing on country of origin, community of origin, and indi-vidual synagogues.

What you need to know:

1. The Jewish community is primarily divided into Ashkenazic and Sephardic Jews, although these dis-tinctions have less and less significance. Most Jews whose families come from Europe are regarded as Ashkenazim, and those whose families come from either Spain or the Arab world are called Sephardim.

2. Today, Sephardic Jews constitute a vital force in world Jewry and a majority in Israeli Jewry.

3. There are numerous differences in the religious and cultural practices of Ashkenazic and Sephardic Jews. What follows is a list of some of the better-known dif-ferences:

Custom	Sephardim	Ashkenazim
Hebrew Pronunciation	Pronounce ת as "t" and ָ as "ah"	Pronounce ת as "s" and ָ as "aw"
Naming	Name children after living relatives	Name after relatives who have died
Torah	Torah kept in hard wooden case and is read standing upright	Torah kept in soft fabric cover and read lying flat on table
Ark	Ark is kept open with Torah scrolls exposed	Ark is covered with a *parochet* (curtain)
Tefillin	Wrapped clockwise	Wrapped counter-clockwise

Language	Ladino	Yiddish
Nusach (chanting of liturgy)	Use distinct nusach derived from Spanish and Near Eastern cultures	Use distinct nusach derived from European cultures
Bar Mitzvah	Celebrate Yom Tefillin First time a boy puts on tefillin For two years prior to a Bar Mitzvah	Observed by boys and girls
Wedding	Bride and groom stand together wrapped in single tallit	Bride and groom stand separately
Shiva	*Keriah* (rending of garments) is done upon return from cemetery Mourners sit on floors or pillows At end of *shiva* a special meal and study session, called a *mishmara* is held	*Keriah* is done at funeral parlor Mourners sit on low stools No special meal served at shiva's end
Foods	Favor spicy Near Eastern delicacies	Favor well-cooked meals and rich cakes
Name for Torah receptacle	Heichal	Aron HaKodesh
Name for yearly anniversary remembrance of loved one	Anos	Yahrzeit

Things to remember:

It is estimated that worldwide, some 80 percent of all Jews are *Ashkenazim,* and only 20 percent *Sephardim.* In the United States, *Ashkenazim* outnumber *Sephardim* by an even greater percentage. In Israel, more than half of the Jewish population is Sephardic.

More Particulars

Who's Who Among Sephardic Jewry
Many notable figures in history boasted Sephardic heritage. Here is a brief listing:

Solomon ibn Gabirol: Poet of the Golden Age of Spain, his works served as models for later poets and also have become part of the High Holy Day liturgy.

Yehoram Gaon: One of Israel's leading entertainers has made his mark as a singer and movie star both in Israel and in the United States.

Judah HaLevi: As a poet/philosopher, he became an inspiration to all the Jews of Spain. His best-known works are *Ode to Zion* and *The Kuzari*.

Joseph Karo: The author of the *Shulchan Arukh*, considered Judaism's most authoritative law code.

Moshe Katzav: The first Sephardic president of the State of Israel.

David Levy: Was the first serious contender of Sephardic descent for the Israeli Prime Minister's position. He narrowly lost out to Yitzchak Shamir in the wake of Prime Minister Begin's resignation.

Moses Maimonides: Also known as Rabbi Moshe ben Maimon (the Rambam), he was born in Cordova in 1135. His great works include *Guide for the Perplexed* and the *Mishneh Torah*.

Joseph Nasi: He spent much time traveling with his aunt Gracia Mendes before rising to power in his own right as an advisor to the Turkish sultan. He used his influence to help his people, including the resettlement of Jewish refugees in Palestine.

Hasdai ibn Shaprut: Living in 10th century Spain, this court physician rose to high government office and used his position to influence policy for the good of the people.

Naomi Shemer: Israel's foremost contemporary songwriter, she is the child of an Ashkenazi/Sephardi marriage. Her most well-known song is probably *Yerushalayim Shel Zahav* (Jerusalem of Gold), released just after the Six-Day War in 1967.

Key words and phrases

Ladino: Spanish-Jewish folk language

If you want to know more:

Robert Sugar, *Our Story: The Jews of Sepharad*. New York: Coalition for the Advancement of Jewish Education, 1991.

Joseph Teleushkin, *Jewish Literacy*. New York: William Morrow, 1991.

Instant Information
Twenty-Year Calendar of Jewish Holidays

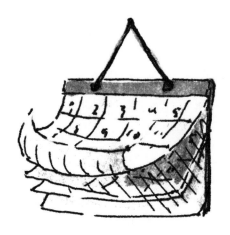

The source:

The Jewish calendar, established by Hillel II in 350 C.E.

What you need to know:

1. While many people think that the Jewish calendar is a lunar calendar, it is really a soli-lunar calendar. This means that it is a lunar calendar that is adjusted by the seasons (which are governed by the sun). This approach prevents holidays from occurring in different seasons each year—as they do in the calendar of Islam. As a result, the Jewish calendar has 354 days, while the secular (solar) calendar has 365 days. Thus, Jewish holidays fall on different days of the secular calendar each year. That's where we get the expression "The holidays are late—or early—this year."

2. Jews in Israel observe one-day festivals, as the Torah prescribes, and continue to do so to this day (except for Rosh Hashanah). The Orthodox and Conservative movements insist that Jews in the Diaspora observe two days of all the holy days. Reform Judaism generally consider such double celebrations unnecessary. However, some congregations have chosen to observe a second day of holidays in order to celebrate at the same time as does the rest of the Jewish world and to increase the opportunities for celebration and observance.

3. Jewish holidays begin in the evening with sunset. This is based on the biblical verse in the story of creation which states that "there was evening and then there was morning."

4. Twenty-Year Calendar of Jewish Holidays:

(dates are listed for the first day of multiple-day holidays only)

2001/5762

Rosh Hashanah	Sept. 18
Yom Kippur	Sept. 27
Sukkot	Oct. 2
Hanukkah	Dec. 10

2002

Purim	Feb. 26
Passover	March 28
Shavuot	May 17

2002/5763

Rosh Hashanah	Sept. 7
Yom Kippur	Sept. 16
Sukkot	Sept. 21
Hanukkah	Nov. 30

2003

Purim	March 18
Passover	April 17
Shavuot	June 6

2003/5764

Rosh Hashanah	Sept. 27
Yom Kippur	Oct. 6
Sukkot	Oct. 11
Hanukkah	Dec. 20

2004

Purim	March 7
Passover	April 6
Shavuot	May 26

2004/5765

| Rosh Hashanah | Sept. 16 |
| Yom Kippur | Sept. 25 |

| Sukkot | Sept. 30 |
| Hanukkah | Dec. 8 |

2005

Purim	March 25
Passover	April 24
Shavuot	June 13

2005/5766

Rosh Hashanah	Oct. 4
Yom Kippur	Oct. 13
Sukkot	Oct. 18
Hanukkah	Dec. 26

2006

Purim	March 14
Passover	April 13
Shavuot	June 2

2006/5767

Rosh Hashanah	Sept. 23
Yom Kippur	Oct. 2
Sukkot	Oct. 7
Hanukkah	Dec. 16

2007

Purim	March 4
Passover	April 3
Shavuot	May 23

2007/5768

Rosh Hashanah	Sept. 13
Yom Kippur	Sept. 22
Sukkot	Sept. 27
Hanukkah	Dec. 5

2008

Purim	March 21
Passover	April 20
Shavuot	June 9

2008/5769

Rosh Hashanah	Sept. 30
Yom Kippur	Oct. 9
Sukkot	Oct. 14
Hanukkah	Dec. 22

2009

Purim	March 10
Passover	April 9
Shavuot	May 21

2010/5770

Rosh Hashanah	Sept. 19
Yom Kippur	Sept. 28
Sukkot	Oct. 3
Hanukkah	Dec. 12

2010

Purim	Feb. 28
Passover	March 30
Shavuot	May 19

2010/5771

Rosh Hashanah	Sept. 9
Yom Kippur	Sept. 18
Sukkot	Sept. 23
Hanukkah	Dec. 2

2011

Purim	March 20
Passover	April 19
Shavuot	June 8

2011/5772

Rosh Hashanah	Sept 29
Yom Kippur	Oct 8
Sukkot	Oct. 13
Hanukkah	Dec. 21

2012

Purim	March 8
Passover	April 7
Shavuot	May 27

2012/5773

Rosh Hashanah	Sept. 17
Yom Kippur	Sept. 26
Sukkot	Oct. 1
Hanukkah	Dec. 9

2013

Purim	Feb. 14
Passover	March 26
Shavuot	May 15

2013/5774

Rosh Hashanah	Sept. 5
Yom Kippur	Sept. 14
Sukkot	Sept. 19
Hanukkah	Dec. 28

2014

Purim	March 16
Passover	April 15
Shavuot	June 4

2014/5775

Rosh Hashanah	Sept. 25
Yom Kippur	Oct. 4
Sukkot	Oct. 9
Hanukkah	Dec. 17

2015

Purim	March 5
Passover	April 4
Shavuot	May 24

2015/5776

Rosh Hashanah	Sept. 14
Yom Kippur	Sept 23
Sukkot	Sept. 28
Hanukkah	Dec. 7

2016

Purim	March 24
Passover	April 23
Shavuot	June 12

2016/5777

Rosh Hashanah	Oct. 3
Yom Kippur	Oct. 12
Sukkot	Oct. 17
Hanukkah	Dec. 25

2017

Purim	March 12
Passover	April 11
Shavuot	May 31

2017/5778

Rosh Hashanah	Sept. 21
Yom Kippur	Sept. 30
Sukkot	Oct. 5
Hanukkah	Dec. 13

2018

Purim	March 1
Passover	March 31
Shavuot	May 20

2018/5779

Rosh Hashanah	Sept. 10
Yom Kippur	Sept. 19
Sukkot	Sept. 24
Hanukkah	Dec. 3

2019

Purim	March 21
Passover	April 20
Shavuot	June 9

2019/5780

Rosh Hashanah	Sept. 30
Yom Kippur	Oct. 9
Sukkot	Oct. 14
Hanukkah	Dec. 23

2020

Purim	March 10
Passover	April 19
Shavuot	May 29

2020/5781

Rosh Hashanah	Sept. 19
Yom Kippur	Sept. 28
Sukkot	Oct. 3
Hanukkah	Dec. 11

Key words and phrases:

Luach: Calendar

If you want to know more:

Kerry M. Olitzky and Ronald H. Isaacs, *Rediscovering Judaism: Bar and Bat Mitzvah for Adults*. Hoboken, NJ: KTAV Publishing House, Inc., 1997.

More particulars:

If an American Jew travels to Israel, he or she must follow the diaspora observance pattern (regarding one- or two-day holidays) unless he or she is going to be there for all three pilgrimage festivals. However, since it is permissible "to extend holiness," Israeli Jews who are going to be outside Israel may extend their observance of the holidays. Nevertheless, most authorities suggest that Israelis who will be abroad on the second day of holidays should put on *tefillin* at home and not at the synagogue.

Instant Information
Sabbath Table Songs

The source:

"When Jewish people eat and drink, they begin with words of Torah and hymns of praise" (Babylonian Talmud, *Megillah* 12b).

What you need to know

1. *Zemirot* (table songs) sung during Sabbath meals provide us with the atmosphere to promote Sabbath joy. They add light and joy to the soul. Since Sabbath table songs are unique, they help to create Jewish memories for our children and ourselves. Composed at an early date, these songs became particularly popular during the 16th century through the influence of the mystics.

2. The tunes of the *zemirot*, reflecting the experiences of Jewish people throughout history, are mostly adapted local folk tunes that eventually became characteristically Jewish.

3. Some popular *zemirot* for you to sing at your Sabbath dinner table:

מְנוּחָה וְשִׂמְחָה אוֹר לַיְּהוּדִים,

יוֹם שַׁבָּתוֹן יוֹם מַחֲמַדִּים,

שׁוֹמְרָיו וְזוֹכְרָיו הֵמָּה מְעִידִים,

כִּי לְשִׁשָּׁה כֹּל בְּרוּאִים וְעוֹמְדִים.

שְׁמֵי שָׁמַיִם אֶרֶץ וְיַמִּים,

כָּל צְבָא מָרוֹם גְּבוֹהִים וְרָמִים,

תַּנִּין וְאָדָם וְחַיַּת רְאֵמִים,

כִּי בְּיָהּ יְיָ צוּר עוֹלָמִים.

1. *Menukha V'simcha*
Menukha v'simcha
Or la-y'udim

Yom Shabbaton yom machmadim
Shomrav v'zochrave heima m'idim
Ki l'shisha b'rurim v'omdim.
Sh'mei shamayim eretz v'yamim
Kol tz'va marom g'vohim v'ramim
Tanim v'adam v'chayat r'eimim
Ki b'yah Adonai tzur olamim.

To rest and rejoice is a Jewish right,
This Sabbath day of sheer delight
Those who keep it say this Friday night
In six days God made the mighty world
The highest heavens, earth and sea,
The angels above, in majesty,
Monsters and humans and beasts running free,
The strengths of the world, Almighty is God.

צוּר מִשֶּׁלּוֹ

צוּר מִשֶּׁלּוֹ אָכַלְנוּ, בָּרְכוּ אֱמוּנַי
שָׂבַעְנוּ וְהוֹתַרְנוּ כִּדְבַר יְיָ.
הַזָּן אֶת עוֹלָמוֹ, רוֹעֵנוּ אָבִינוּ, אָכַלְנוּ
אֶת לַחְמוֹ, וְיֵינוֹ שָׁתִינוּ, עַל כֵּן נוֹדֶה
לִשְׁמוֹ, וּנְהַלְלוֹ בְּפִינוּ, אָמַרְנוּ וְעָנִינוּ,
אֵין קָדוֹשׁ כַּיְיָ.

2. *Tzur Mishelo*
Tzur mishelo achalnu
Bar'khu emunai
Savanu v'hotarnu kidvar Adonai
Hazan et olamo, ro-einu avinu
Akhalnu et lachmo v'yeinu shatinu,
Al ken nodeh lishmo un-hal'lo b'finu
Amarnu v'aninu ein kadosh kadonai.

We've eaten God's food; let's adore and bless God in
   one accord
We've had enough and more, by the word of God.
God keeps the world well fed, this Shepherd Parent of
   mine
We ate God's tasty bread and drank God's goodly wine
Let's thank God, feeling glad, and praise God as
   we dine,
Singing as we recline: None is holy like God.

דְּרוֹר יִקְרָא לְבֵן עִם בַּת. וְיִנְצָרְכֶם
כְּמוֹ בָבַת. נְעִים שִׁמְכֶם וְלֹא
יִשְׁבַּת. שְׁבוּ וְנוּחוּ בְּיוֹם שַׁבָּת.
דְּרוֹשׁ נָוִי וְאוּלָמִי. וְאוֹת יֶשַׁע עֲשֵׂה
עִמִּי. נְטַע שׂוֹרֵק בְּתוֹךְ כַּרְמִי. שְׁעֵה
שַׁוְעַת בְּנֵי עַמִּי.

3. *Dror Yikra*

D'ror yikra, l'vein ul-vat
V'yin tzorkhem k'mo vavat,
N'im shimkhem v'lo yushbat,
Sh'vu v'nu'chu b'yom Shabbat.
D'rosh navi v'ulami
V'ot yesha asei imi,
N'ta soreik b'tokh karmi
Sh'ei shav'at b'nei ami.

God invites God's children to partake of Shabbat
To rest from labor, anxiety, and strife.
Shabbat renews the heart, inspires wisdom,
And restores dignity of life.
God will proclaim freedom for all the children
And will keep you as the apple of God's eye
Pleasant is your name and will not be destroyed
Repose and rest on the Sabbath day.

מִפִּי אֵל

מִפִּי אֵל מִפִּי אֵל יְבֹרַךְ יִשְׂרָאֵל
אֵין אַדִּיר כַּיְיָ, אֵין בָּרוּךְ כְּבֶן עַמְרָם,
אֵין גְּדוּלָה כַּתּוֹרָה, אֵין דּוֹרְשֶׁיהָ
כְּיִשְׂרָאֵל.

4. *Mipi Eil*

Mipi Eil mipi Eil
Y'vorakh yisrael.
Ein adir kadonai
Ein barukh k'ven amram
Ein g'dolah katorah
Ein dorsheha k'yisrael.

There is no other as powerful as God,
None as blessed as Moses, the son of Amram.
There is no other as great as the Torah
And who profess, as Israel.
God will bless Israel.

לֹא יִשָׂא גוֹי

לֹא יִשָׂא גוֹי אֶל גוֹי חֶרֶב
וְלֹא יִלְמְדוּ עוֹד מִלְחָמָה.
לֹא יִשָׂא גוֹי אֶל גוֹי חֶרֶב
וְלֹא יִלְמְדוּ עוֹד מִלְחָמָה.

5. *Lo Yisa Goy*
Lo yisa goy el goy cherev
Lo yilmedu od milchama
Lo yisa goy el goy cherev
Lo yilmedu od milchama

Nation shall not lift up sword against nation
Neither shall we learn war anymore.

Key words and phrases:

Zemer (plural, *Zemirot*): Sabbath and Festival hymns

If you want to know more

Ronald Isaacs, *Every Person's Guide to Shabbat*. Northvale, NJ: Jason Aronson, 1998.

_____, *Shabbat Delight: A Celebration in Stories, Games and Songs*. Hoboken, NJ and New York: KTAV and the American Jewish Committee, 1987.

Instant Information
Healing Prayers

The source:

"O God, heal her now" (Numbers 12:13).

What you need to know:

1. The obligation to heal in Jewish tradition dates back to biblical times, when prayers were used in time of illness. Abraham prayed for the recovery of Avimelech (Gen. 20:17) and God healed him. Moses prayed for the recovery of his sister Miriam with the words "O God, heal her now." (Numbers 12:13) and she recovered from (what most commentators say was) leprosy. This short, simple prayer became the model for all prayers.

2. Years ago, the 18th-century Hasidic master Rabbi Nachman of Bratslav identified ten specific psalms that have inherent power to bring a true and complete healing of both body and spirit. He designated the ten psalms (numbers 16, 32, 41, 42, 59, 77, 90, 105, 137, 150) as a *Tikkun Haklali*—the Complete Remedy. (See Healing Psalms section in Instant Information for the complete texts of these psalms.)

3. Since the *mi sheberakh* requires a *minyan*, it is generally said while the congregation is engaged in the Torah service, following an *aliyah*.

4. Some congregations offer *mi sheberakh* prayers individually. Others offer them on behalf of all those who are ill.

4. The prayer takes its name from the first two words— *mi sheberakh*, "the One who blessed," namely God. While most people use this name to refer to the prayer for healing, there are a variety of *mi sheberakh* prayers. What they share in common is a request of God to bless a specific person or persons. Besides healing, they ask God to reward various individuals including those who have come up for the Torah

reading, those who make donations to the synagogue and other worthy causes, bar and bat mitzvah celebrants, wedding celebrants, and those who have been circumcised and/or named.

5. There are many prayers found in the *siddur,* the Bible, and in contemporary writings that include healing prayers and texts. Some common examples:

    i. Praised are You, Sovereign our God, Ruler of the Universe, who with wisdom fashioned the human body, creating openings, arteries, glands and organs, marvelous in structure, intricate in design. Should but one of them, by being blocked, fail to function, it would be impossible to exist. Praised are You, God, Healer of all flesh, who sustains our bodies in wondrous ways. (From the liturgy, *Asher Yatzar*)

    ii. Our Parent, Our Sovereign, send complete healing to those who are ill. (From the liturgy, *Avinu Malkenu*)

    iii. May God who blessed our ancestors Abraham, Isaac and Jacob, Sarah, Rebecca, Rachel and Leah, bless and heal _____. May the Holy One in kindness strengthen him (her) and heal him (her) speedily, body and soul, together with all others who are ill.

    iv. O God, I turn to You in prayer,
You who bind up wounds and heal the sick.
I put my trust in You.
Knowing that I am in Your hands, O God,
I have faith that You will not forsake me.
Give me courage now and in the days ahead,
Grant wisdom and skill to my physician.
Make all those who are assisting me
Instruments of Your healing power.
Give me strength for this day
And grant me hope for tomorrow.
Hear my prayer, be with me and protect me.
Restore me to health, O God
So that I may serve You. (Prayer before an operation)

    vi. Hear my voice O God, when I call,
Be gracious to me and answer me. (Psalm 27:7)

vii. Heal me, O God, and I shall be healed.
   Saved me and I shall be saved;
   For You are my praise. (Jeremiah 17:14)

Things to remember:

1. The *mi sheberakh* should be said in the context of a community. Thus, a *minyan* is required.

2. The person for whom the *mi sheberakh* is said is mentioned as the son or daughter of his or her mother (rather than father as is the case in most other traditional Jewish contexts).

Key words and phrases:

Mi sheberakh: (May) The One who blesses . . .
Refuah shleima: complete healing (used as an expression from one person to another, often when speaking of a third person)

If you want to know more:

David L. Freeman and Judith Z. Abrams, eds., *Illness and Healing in the Jewish Tradition: Writings from the Bible to Today*. Philadelphia: Jewish Publication Society of America, 1999.

Ronald Isaacs, *A Gabbai's How To Manual*. Hoboken, NJ: KTAV Publishing, 1996.

————, *Judaism, Medicine and Healing*. Northvale, NJ: Jason Aronson, 1998.

Kerry M. Olitzky, *Jewish Paths to Healing and Wholeness*. Woodstock, VT: Jewish Lights Publishing, 2000.

Simkha Y. Weintraub, ed., *Healing of Soul, Healing of Body*. Woodstock, VT: Jewish Lights Publishing, 1994.

The source:

"Study is the most basic *mitzvah* of them all" (Babylonian Talmud, *Shabbat* 127a).

What you need to know:

1. Mohammed is credited with naming the Jews "the People of the Book." From the days of Ezra, the Torah and the books added to it were so intimately a part of the Jewish people that they could not easily conceive of another way of life. Not even the king was exempt from reading and studying the Torah.

2. The life and destiny of the Jewish people was formed not only by the Bible but also by the many volumes that were inspired by the Bible, including both classic and contemporary texts.

3. Following are some suggestions for your home library and your reading table:

Basic Reference

Kerry M. Olitzky and Ronald Isaacs, *A Glossary of Jewish Life*. Northvale, NJ: Jason Aronson, 1992.

Life Cycle

Ronald Isaacs, *Rites of Passage: A Guide to the Jewish Life Cycle*. Hoboken, NJ: KTAV, 1992. (Conservative)
Isaac Klein, *A Guide to Jewish Religious Practice*. New York and Jerusalem: Jewish Theological Seminary of America, 1979, 1992. (Conservative)
Simeon J. Maslin, ed., *Gates of Mitzvah: A Guide to the Jewish Life Cycle*. New York: Central Conference of American Rabbis, 1979. (Reform)

Philosophy/Theology

Eugene B. Borowitz, *Choices in Modern Jewish Thought: A Partisan Guide*. New York: Behrman House, 1983.

Elliot Dorff, *Knowing God*. Northvale, NJ: Jason Aronson, 1992.

Neil Gillman, *Sacred Fragments: Recovering Theology for the Modern Jew*. Philadelphia: Jewish Publication Society, 1990.

Ronald Isaacs, *Every Person's Guide to Jewish Philosophy and Philosophers*. Northvale, NJ: Jason Aronson, 1999.

Harold Kushner, *When Bad Things Happen to Good People*. New York: Schocken, 1981.

_____, *When Children Ask About God*. New York: Schocken, 1976.

Daniel Syme, *Finding God*. New York: Union of American Hebrew Congregations, 1986.

Bibles with Commentary

Bernard Bamberger, William W. Hallo, and W. Gunther Plaut, eds., *The Torah: A Modern Commentary*. New York: Union of American Hebrew Congregations, 1981. (Reform)

Joseph H. Hertz, *Pentateuch and Haftorahs*. New York: Soncino Press, 1988. (Traditional)

The J.P.S. Commentary. 5 volumes. Philadelphia: Jewish Publication Society, 1996.

Prayer Books

Jules Harlow, ed., *Siddur Sim Shalom*. New York: Rabbinical Assembly and United Synagogue of America, 1985. (Conservative)

Joseph H. Hertz, ed., *Authorized Daily Prayer Book*. New York: Bloch, 1961. (Traditional)

Chaim Stern, ed., *Gates of Prayer*. New York: Central Conference of American Rabbis, 1972. (Reform)

David Teutsch, ed., *Kol Haneshama*. Wyncote, PA.: Reconstructionist Press, 1994. (Reconstructionist)

Text Study

Barry Holtz., ed., *Back to the Sources: Reading the Classic Jewish Text*. New York: Summit Books, 1984.

Michael Katz and Gershon Schwartz, *Swimming in the Sea of Talmud*. Philadelphia: Jewish Publication Society, 1997.

Leonard Kravitz and Kerry M. Olitzky, *Pirke Avot: A Modern Commentary on Jewish Ethics*. New York: UAHC Press, 1993.

_____, *Shemonah Perakim: A Treatise on the Soul*. New York: UAHC Press, 1999.

Holiday and Festival Observances

Penina V. Adelman, *Rituals for Jewish Women Around the Year*. New York: Biblio Press, 1986.

Nahum N. Glatzer, ed., *The Passover Haggadah*. New York: Schocken, 1981.

Philip Goodman, ed., *The Passover, Purim, Rosh Hashanah, Shavuot, Sukkot and Simchat Torah* and *Yom Kippur Anthologies*. 6 volumes. Philadelphia: Jewish Publication Society, 1970–1973.

Kerry M. Olitzky, *Eight Nights, Eight Lights: Family Values for Hanukkah*. Los Angeles: Alef Design Group, 1994.

_____ and Ronald Isaacs, *Sacred Celebrations*. Hoboken, NJ: KTAV, 1994.

Ron Wolfson, *The Art of Jewish Living: Hanukkah*. New York: Federation of Jewish Men's Clubs, 1990.

_____, *The Art of Jewish Living: Passover*. New York and Los Angeles: Federation of Jewish Men's Clubs and University of Judaism, 1988.

_____, *The Art of Jewish Living: The Shabbat Seder*. New York and Los Angeles: Federation of Jewish Men's Clubs and University of Judaism, 1985.

General History

Abba Eban, *Heritage: Civilization and the Jews*. New York: Summit Books, 1984.

Steven Bayme, *Understanding Jewish History: Texts and Commentaries*. Hoboken, NJ: KTAV, 1997.

Paul Johnson, *A History of the Jews*. New York: Harper and Row, 1987.

Abram Leon Sachar, *A History of the Jews*. New York: Knopf, 1967.

Israel

Abraham Joshua Heschel, *Israel: An Echo of Eternity*. New York: Farrar, Straus and Giroux, 1969.

Howard Morley Sachar, *A History of Israel: From the Rise of Zionism to Our Time*. New York, Knopf, 1976.

Sol Scharfstein, *Understanding Israel*. Hoboken, NJ: KTAV, 1994.

The American Jewish Experience

Nathan Glazer, *American Judaism*. 2nd edition. Chicago: University of Chicago Press, 1972.

Jacob Rader Marcus, *United States Jewry, 1776–1985*. Detroit: Wayne State University Press, 1989.

Key words and phrases:

Am hasefer: People of the book

Instant Information
Avoiding *Lashon Hara*

The source:

You shall not go about spreading slander among your people. (Leviticus 19:16)

What you need to know:

1. Words can be powerful objects. When used properly, they can soothe and comfort. However, when they are used improperly, they can hurt, injure and curse. The power of words was described this way in the book of Proverbs: "Death and life are in the power of the tongue." (18:21)

2. Words are used so frivolously at times that we do not often stop to think about them and the way in which they ought to be used. Taking them for granted, we often value their power less than we should.

3. The specific vice of slander is condemned in all Jewish writings. The term slander (*lashon hara*) has been defined as the utterance or dissemination of false statements or reports concerning a person, or malicious representation of that person's actions, in order to defame or injure. According to the Talmud, it is a hideous crime which can easily destroy a person's life and reputation.

4. A cross-section of practical advice culled from a variety of Jewish sources to help prevent you from engaging in *lashon hara*:

   i. **Don't speak too much**: "A person should try to discipline himself not to speak too much so that he should not come to the point of uttering *lashon hara* or indecent words and should not become a chronic complainer. Instead, he should stress silence." (*Menorat HaMaor*)

   ii. **Keep a civil tongue**: "A person should always try to keep a civil tongue in his head, whether engaged in Torah study or discussing worldly affairs." (*Menorat HaMaor*)

iii. **Study Torah**: "If your tongue turns to uttering slander, go and study the words of Torah." (Midrash on Psalms)

iv. **Put your hands in your ears**: "If you hear something unseemly, you should put your hands in your ears." (Babylonian Talmud, *Ketubot* 5a-b)

Key words and phrases:

Lashon hara: Slander

If you want to know more:

Ronald Isaacs, *The Jewish Book of Etiquette*. Northvale, NJ: Jason Aronson, 1998.

Zelig Pliskin, *A Practical Guide to the Laws of Loshon Hara Based on Chofetz Chayim*. Jerusalem: NP, 1975.

Yehudah HeChasid, *The Book of the Pious*. Northvale, NJ: Jason Aronson, 1997.

Basic Terms in Kabbalah

The source:

Kabbalah is the term generally used to describe the esoteric teachings of Judaism and Jewish mysticism. It literally means the "received tradition."

What you need to know:

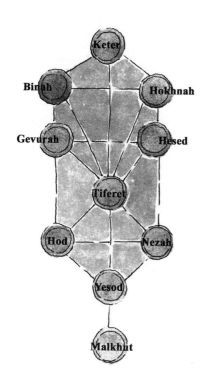

Adam kadmon: primordial man, the first human spiritual prototype

Bittul hayesh: annihilation of individuality, through direct communion with God

Devekut: spiritual communion with God, where the ego is nearly annihilated

Ein Sof: the Infinite, a name for God

Hitbodedut: solitude, being alone with God

Histavvut: equanimity, the indifference of the soul to praise or blame

Kavannah: meditative verses, or the attitude or intent with which one does something

Kelippot (*kelippah*, sing.): husks or shells of evil that were embedded in the earth following creation

Nitzotzot: sparks of holiness that need to be released from the earth

Orot: lights of holiness

Sefirot (*sefirah*, sing.): mystical emanations of God, an idea influenced by I Chronicles 29:11

> *Keter* (*elyon*): (supreme) crown
> *Chokhmah*: wisdom
> *Da'at*: knowledge
> *Binah*: intelligence
> *Gedulah* (or *chesed*): greatness (or love)
> *Gevurah* (or *din*): power (or judgment)
> *Tiferet* (or *rachamim*): beauty (or compassion)
> *Netzah*: lasting endurance
> *Hod*: majesty

tzadik or (*yesod olam*): righteous one or foundation of
the world

malkhut (or *atarah*): sovereignty (or diadem)

Shekhinah: God's indwelling presence, and feminine
attributes

shemittot (*shemittah*, sing.): cosmic cycles

shevirat kelim: breaking of the vessels at creation

sitra achra: the other side, the domain of dark emanations
and demonic powers

tikkun: repair of the world (and of the self)

tzimtzum: contraction of God for the purpose of creation
of the world

Things to remember:

While kabbalah is one of many terms referring to mysticism (from the 14th century on), the Talmud speaks of *sitrei Torah* and *razei Torah* (both, secrets of the Torah). Parts of this secret tradition are called *ma'aseh bereishit* (literally, the work of creation) and *ma'aseh merkabah* (work of the chariot).

Key words and phrases:

Anshei emunah: men of belief

Ba'alei hasod: masters of mystery, a mystical group during
the period following the close of the Talmud

Ba'alei hayediah: masters of knowledge

Chokhmah: wisdom, part of the inner truth

Chokhmah penimit: inner wisdom, from the period of the
Provencal and Spanish kabbalists

Chokhmat ha-emet: the science of truth

Chokhmat hatzeruf: meditations on letter combinations

Chokhmei halev: the wise-hearted, following Exodus 28:3

Derekh ha-emet: the way of truth

Emet: truth, the inner truth

Emunah: faith, part of the inner truth

Hayodim: those who know

Maskilim: the enlightened ones, a reference to Daniel
12:10, not be confused with those of the later
Enlightenment period

Yordei merkabah: those who descend to the chariot, the name of a mystical group

If you want to know more:

David S. Ariel, *The Mystic Quest: An Introduction to Jewish Mysticism*. Northvale, NJ: Jason Aronson, 1988.
David A. Cooper, *God Is a Verb*. New York: Riverhead Books, 1997.

More particulars:

The Zohar (ca. 1280) is the core book in Jewish mysticism and is a commentary or midrash on the Torah. However, there are other mystical volumes, such as *Sefer Yetzirah* (ca. 1130).

The source:

Babylonian Talmud.

What you need to know:

There are six orders or sections of the Babylonian Talmud. These are divided into sections called tractates, sometimes referred to as books. Next to the Hebrew name is the subject matter (in parentheses). An asterisk means that this tractate appears in the Talmud of Eretz Yisrael (the land of Israel), inaccurately called by most people the Jerusalem Talmud, as well. However, the material may not be the same.

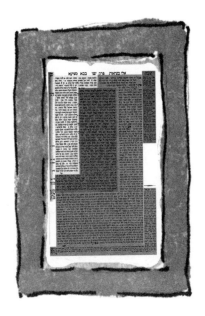

Seder Zeraim
Berakhot (blessings)*
Peah (gleanings of the field)*
Demai (doubtfully tithed produce)*
Kilayim (diverse kinds)*
Shevi'it (Sabbatical year)*
Terumot (heave offering)*
Ma'aserot (tithes)*
Ma'aser Sheni (second tithe)*
Challah (dough offering)*
Orlah (the fruit of young trees)*
Bikkurim (first fruits)*

Seder Moed
Shabbat (Sabbath)*
Eruvim (Sabbath limits)*
Pesachim (Passover)*
Shekalim (shekel dues)*
Yoma (Day of Atonement)*
Sukkah (Feast of Tabernacles)*
Beitzah (festival laws)*
Rosh Hashanah (various new years)*
Ta'anit (fast days)*
Megillah (Purim)*

Moed Katan (intermediate days of festivals)*
Chagigah (festival offering)*

Seder Nashim
Yevamot (levirate marriage)*
Ketubot (marriage contracts)*
Nedarim (vows)*
Nazir (the Nazirite)*
Sotah (one suspected of adultery)*
Gittin (divorce)*
Kiddushin (marriage)*

Seder Nezikin
Bava Kamma (torts)*
Bava Metziah (civil law)*
Bava Batra (property law)*
Sanhedrin (judges and courts)*
Makkot (flagellation)*
Shevuot (oaths)*
Eduyyot (traditional testimonies)
Avodah Zarah (idolatry)*
Avot (ethical maxims)
Horayot (erroneous rulings of the court)*

Seder Kodashim
Zevachim (animal offerings)
Menachot (meal offerings)
Chullin (animals slaughtered for food)
Bekhorot (firstlings)
Arakin (vows of valuation)
Temurah (substituted offering)
Keritot (extirpation)
Me'ilah (sacrileges)
Tamid (the daily sacrifice)
Middot (measurements of the Temple)
Kinnim (the bird offering)

Seder Tohorot
Kelim (uncleanness of articles)
Oholot (uncleanness through overshadowing)
Negaim (leprosy)
Parah (the red heifer)
Tohorot (ritual cleanness)
Mikvaot (ritual ablution)
Niddah (the menstruant)*

Makhshirin (liquid that predisposes food to become ritually unclean)

Zavim (fluxes)

Tevul Yom (ritual uncleanness between immersion and sunset)

Yadayim (ritual uncleanness of the hands)

Uktzin ("stalks"; part of plant that is susceptible to uncleanness)

Things to remember:

1. Pages of the Talmud are numbered on both sides of the page: A, then B.

2. Because the cover is counted as a page, each book starts on page two.

Key words and phrases:

Talmud means "study" or "learning." It refers to a specific collection of oral law (either the Babylonian or Eretz Yisrael/Jerusalem Talmud)—the body of teaching that comprises the commentary and discussions of the rabbis on the mishnah compiled by Rabbi Judah Hanasi. It can also refer to the whole body of one's learning (in much the same way that the word Torah is used). It can also be used as part of a technical phrase regarding a teaching that emerges from a Biblical text (as in *talmud lomar*). Alternatively, the Talmud is called *shas*, an acronym for *shisah sidrei* (the six orders of the mishnah) or *gemara* (the specific Aramaic commentary/discussion on the mishnah).

If you want to know more:

Michael Katz and Gershon Schwartz, *Swimming in the Sea of Talmud: Lessons for Everyday Living*. Philadelphia: Jewish Publication Society of America, 1997.

We have included Biblical sources for each of the following selected tractates for which its Torah source is readily ascertained. Not all tractates are listed below.

Seder Zeraim
Peah (see Lev. 19:9–10)
Kitayim (see Deut. 22:9–11)

Shevi'it (see Exod. 23:10–11)
Terumot (see Lev. 22:10–14)
Ma'aserot (see Num. 18:21)
Ma'aser Sheni (see Deut. 14:22ff.)
Challah (see Num. 15:17–21)
Orlah (see Lev. 19:23–25)
Bikkurim (see Lev. 26:1–11)

Seder Moed
Shekalim (see Exod. 30:11–16)
Chagigah (see Deut. 16:16–17)

Seder Nashim
Yevamot (see Deut. 25:5–10)
Nedarim (see Num. 30)
Nazir (see Num. 6)
Sotah (see Num. 5:11ff.)

Seder Nezikin
Makkot (see Deut. 25:2)
Horayot (see Lev. 4:22ff.)

Seder Kodashim
Bekhorot (see Deut. 15:19ff.)
Arakin (see Lev. 27:1–8)
Terumah (see Lev. 27:10)
Keritot (see Lev. 18:29)
Me'ilah (see Lev. 5:15–16)
Tamid (see Num. 28:3–4)
Kinnim (see Lev. 5:7ff.)

Seder Tohorot
Oholot (see Num. 19:14–15)
Negaim (see Lev. 13, 14)
Parah (see Num. 19)
Makhshirin (see Lev. 11:37–38)
Zavim (see Lev. 15)
Tevul Yom (see Lev. 22:6–7)

Instant Information
Fifteen Morning Blessings

The source:

Babylonian Talmud, *Berakhot* 60b

What you need to know:

This series of 15 blessings emerges from the Talmud, where the rabbis teach that we should praise God as we experience each activity in a new day. For example, one thanks God for giving us the crucial ability to make various distinctions in life, such as the difference between night and day, when we rub our eyes and see things for the first time in the morning. Some of these activities are obvious from the text of the blessing. Others are not so obvious. Among them are: sitting up and stretching (who has made me to be free); getting out of bed (gives strength to the weary); stands on the floor (established firm ground amidst the waters); putting on shoes, which demonstrates our ability to make our way in the world (provides for all my needs); setting on toward one's destination (makes firm each person's steps); fastening one's clothing (girds Israel with strength); putting on a hat, which reminds us that God is above us (crowns Israel with splendor); feeling the passing of nighttime exhaustion (gives strength to the weary and removes sleep from the eyelids).

Blessings of the Morning

בִּרְכוֹת הַשַּׁחַר

בָּרוּךְ אַתָּה יְיָ אֱלֹהֵינוּ מֶלֶךְ הָעוֹלָם, אֲשֶׁר נָתַן לַשֶּׂכְוִי בִינָה לְהַבְחִין בֵּין יוֹם וּבֵין לָיְלָה.

Barukh ata Adonai Elohenu melekh ha-olam asher natan la-sekhvi vina le-havchin bein yom u'vein laila.

Praised are You, Adonai our God, Sovereign of the Universe, who has given me the ability to distinguish between day and night.

155

בָּרוּךְ אַתָּה יְיָ אֱלֹהֵינוּ מֶלֶךְ הָעוֹלָם, שֶׁעָשַׂנִי בְּצַלְמוֹ.

Barukh ata Adonai Elohenu melekh ha-olam she'asani betzalmo.

Praised are You, Adonai our God, Sovereign of the Universe, who has made me in the Divine image (alt: who has not made me a woman; who has made me according to Divine will).

בָּרוּךְ אַתָּה יְיָ אֱלֹהֵינוּ מֶלֶךְ הָעוֹלָם, שֶׁעָשַׂנִי יִשְׂרָאֵל.

Barukh atah Adonai Elohenu melekh ha-olam she'asani yisrael.

Praised are You, Adonai our God, Sovereign of the Universe, who has led me to my Jewish heritage (alt: who has not made me a Gentile).

בָּרוּךְ אַתָּה יְיָ אֱלֹהֵינוּ מֶלֶךְ הָעוֹלָם, שֶׁעָשַׂנִי בֶּן־ (בַּת־) חוֹרִין.

Barukh atah Adonai Elohenu melekh ha-olam she'asani ben (bat) chorin.

Praised are You, Adonai our God, Sovereign of the Universe, who has made me free (alt: who has not made me a slave).

בָּרוּךְ אַתָּה יְיָ אֱלֹהֵינוּ מֶלֶךְ הָעוֹלָם, פּוֹקֵחַ עִוְרִים.

Barukh atah Adonai Elohenu melekh ha-olam poke'ach ivrim.

Praised are You, Adonai our God, Sovereign of the Universe, who opens the eyes of those who would not see.

בָּרוּךְ אַתָּה יְיָ אֱלֹהֵינוּ מֶלֶךְ הָעוֹלָם, מַלְבִּישׁ עֲרֻמִּים.

Barukh atah Adonai Elohenu melekh ha-olam malbish arumim.

Praised are You, Adonai our God, Sovereign of the Universe, who clothes the naked.

בָּרוּךְ אַתָּה יְיָ אֱלֹהֵינוּ מֶלֶךְ הָעוֹלָם, מַתִּיר אֲסוּרִים.

Barukh atah Adonai Elohenu melekh ha-olam matir asurim.

Praised are You, Adonai our God, Sovereign of the Universe, who brings freedom to the captive.

בָּרוּךְ אַתָּה יְיָ אֱלֹהֵינוּ מֶלֶךְ הָעוֹלָם, זוֹקֵף כְּפוּפִים.

Barukh atah Adonai Elohenu melekh ha-olam zokef kefufim.

Praised are You, Adonai our God, Sovereign of the Universe, who girds us with courage (alt: who straightens the bent).

בָּרוּךְ אַתָּה יְיָ אֱלֹהֵינוּ מֶלֶךְ הָעוֹלָם, רוֹקַע הָאָרֶץ עַל הַמָּיִם.

Barukh atah Adonai Elohenu melekh ha-olam roka ha'aretz al ha-mayim.

Praised are You, Adonai our God, Sovereign of the Universe, who establishes firm ground amidst the waters.

בָּרוּךְ אַתָּה יְיָ אֱלֹהֵינוּ מֶלֶךְ הָעוֹלָם, שֶׁעָשָׂה לִי כָּל צָרְכִּי.

Barukh atah Adonai Elohenu melekh ha-olam she'asah lee kol tzorkee.

Praised are You, Adonai our God, Sovereign of the Universe, who provides for all my needs.

בָּרוּךְ אַתָּה יְיָ אֱלֹהֵינוּ מֶלֶךְ הָעוֹלָם הַמֵּכִין מִצְעֲדֵי גָבֶר.

Barukh atah Adonai Elohenu melekh ha-olam ha-maykhin mitz'adei gaver.

Praised are You, Adonai our God, Sovereign of the Universe, who makes firm each person's steps.

בָּרוּךְ אַתָּה יְיָ אֱלֹהֵינוּ מֶלֶךְ הָעוֹלָם, אוֹזֵר יִשְׂרָאֵל בִּגְבוּרָה.

Barukh atah Adonai Elohenu melekh ha-olam ozer yisrael bigevurah.

Praised are You, Adonai our God, Sovereign of the Universe, who girds Israel with strength.

בָּרוּךְ אַתָּה יְיָ אֱלֹהֵינוּ מֶלֶךְ הָעוֹלָם, עוֹטֵר יִשְׂרָאֵל בְּתִפְאָרָה.

Barukh atah Adonai Elohenu melekh ha-olam oter yisrael be-tifarah.

Praised are You, Adonai our God, Sovereign of the Universe, who crowns Israel with splendor.

בָּרוּךְ אַתָּה יְיָ אֱלֹהֵינוּ מֶלֶךְ הָעוֹלָם, הַנּוֹתֵן לַיָּעֵף כֹּחַ.

Barukh atah Adonai Elohenu melekh ha-olam ha-noten la-aiyef koach.

Praised are You, Adonai our God, Sovereign of the Universe, who gives strength to the weary.

בָּרוּךְ אַתָּה יְיָ אֱלֹהֵינוּ מֶלֶךְ הָעוֹלָם, הַמַּעֲבִיר שֵׁנָה מֵעֵינַי וּתְנוּמָה מֵעַפְעַפָּי.

Barukh atah Adonai Elohenu melekh ha-olam ha'ma'avir sheina may'aynai ut'numah may'afapai.

Praised are You, Adonai our God, Sovereign of the Universe, who removes sleep from my eyes and slumber from my eyelids.

Some *siddurim* attach this additional paragraph to the last blessing:

Yehi ratzon

Yehi ratzon milfanekha Adonai elohenu vaylohay avotaynu she'-targeelaynu betoratekha ve-dabkeinu bemitzvotekha ve'al te'veeyanu lo leeday chet velo leeday aveirah ve'avon velo lee-day neesayon velo leeday veezayon ve'al tashlet banu yetzer ha'ra ve-harcheekaynu may'adam rah u'maychaver rah ve-dabkeinu beyetzer ha-tov uv-ma'asim tovim vechof et yeet-zraynu le-heeshtabed lakh u'tneinu hayom u'vechol yom le-chen ul'chesed ul'rachamim be'aynekha uv'aynay khol

158

ro'aynu ve-teegmelaynu chasadim tovim. Barukh atah Adonai gomel chasadim tovim le'amo yisrael.

May it be your will, Adonai our God, and God of our ancestors, that you accustom us to study the Torah and attach us to your *mitzvot*. Do not bring us into the power of error nor into the orbit of transgression and sin, nor into the influence of challenge, nor be drawn into scorn. Do not let the inclination to do evil dominate us. Distance us from an evil person and an evil companion. Attach us to the inclination to do good and to do good deeds. Compel our inclination to do evil to be subservient to you. Grant us today and every day grace, kindness, and mercy in Your eyes and in the eyes of all who see us, and bestow beneficent kindness upon us. Praised are You, Adonai our God, who bestows kindness on the people Israel.

Things to remember:

1. These blessings should be said while standing.

2. These blessings are said before the morning service and should be recited prior to breakfast.

Key words and phrases:

Barukh ata Adonai Elohenu Melekh ha-Olam is the formula used to initiate a formal blessing. Some prayer books have translated this as "Praised be the Source of Life" in order to avoid any gender reference.

If you want to know more:

Joel Lurie Grishaver, *And You Shall Be a Blessing: An Unfolding of the Six Words That Begin Every Berakhah.* Northvale, NJ: Jason Aronson, Inc., 1994.

Reuven Hammer, *Entering Jewish Prayer: A Guide to Personal Devotion and the Worship Service.* New York: Schocken Books, 1995.

More particulars:

Rabbi Isaac Luria taught that a righteous person should respond to a minimum of 90 blessings each day and recite no less than 100 blessings each day. To assure these 90 Amen responses, some people recite these 15 blessings aloud for one another.

The paragraph attached to the last blessing that begins "May it be Your will" was the personal prayer recited by Rabbi Yehudah Hanasi every day after *shacharit*, according to the Talmud (*Berakhot* 16b). It is a prayer that asks God for divine protection during our everyday dealings with others. One commentator suggests that after its recitation, we should add our personal requests for God's help during the day.

Instant Information
Healing Psalms

The source:

Rabbi Nachman's Psalms of Healing[2] are taken from his *Comprehensive Remedy.*

What you need to know:

Psalm 16
These are among David's golden words:
Watch over me, God,
    for I seek refuge in You.
You said to Adonai:
        "You are my Master,
            but my good fortune is not Your concern.
"Rather, the holy ones on the earth
        —You care for them
        and the great ones who I should emulate.
"When the pain multiplies,
    they know to speedily turn to another,
But I cannot even pour their libations because of guilt,
    I cannot even lift their names to my lips."
Adonai is the Portion, which is mine by right,
    my Cup.
    You nurture my destiny.
Labor pains turn into pleasantness—
    so, too, I must see my inheritance of beauty.
I will bless Adonai who counsels me,
    though at night my conscience afflicts me.
I will keep Adonai continually before me;
    because of God-Who-is-my-Right-Hand,
    I shall not break down.
So my mind is happy,
    my whole being is joyful;
        even my body rests secure.

[2]Translations adapted from Simkha Y. Weintraub, ed., *Healing of Soul, Healing of Body: Spiritual Leaders Unfold the Strength and Solace in Psalms.* Woodstock, VT: Jewish Lights Publishing, 1994.

For You shall not abandon my soul
to the world of the dead,
nor let the one who loves You
see one's own grave.
Give me directions on life's road.
With Your presence,
I am filled with joys,
with the delights that ever come
from Your Strong Arm.

Psalm 32

A Song of David, of instruction:

Happy is one whose sins are forgiven,
whose transgressions are wiped away.
Happy is one whose wrongdoing Adonai passes over,
whose Spirit is without deceit.
When I kept silent, my bones wore out;
I groaned all day in fear.
Day and night Your Hand weighed heavily upon me;
My marrow turned dry, parched as by the heat of
summer,
Selah.
So now, I will acknowledge my transgression,
I will no longer obscure wrongdoing;
Even as I began to say, "I admit my sins
before Adonai,"
You forgave my errors and misdeeds, *Selah.*
Let one devoted to You offer this prayer
at those moments when You may be found:
*"When trials and troubles come,
may they not flood in a deluge of destruction!"*
You are my Shelter,
You protect me from distress, from enemies,
You surround me with the joy of deliverance,
Selah.
(You have said:)
"I will teach you Wisdom,
I will illumine the path you must take,
My eye will advise you and guide you."
Do not be like a horse or a mule who cannot
understand,
who, with a bit and a bridle,

must be restrained during grooming,
>so that they do not come too close and
>>attack.
Many are the troubles of the wicked,
>but one who trusts in Adonai
>>will be enveloped by loving abundance of
>>>kindness.
Rejoice in Adonai!
>Exult, righteous ones!
>>Shout for joy, all who are upright in heart!

Psalm 41

To the Chief Musician: A Song of David

Happy is the one who attends to the needy;
>On an evil day, Adonai will rescue her
Adonai will guard her, Adonai will give her life;
>She will be considered fortunate on this earth,
>>not subject to the whims of enemies.
Adonai will nurture her on her sickbed;
>Even when her illness advances, and her rest is
>>disturbed,
>You will attend to her and turn things around.
As for me, I said,
>"Adonai, have pity;
>Heal my soul, for I have sinned against You."
My enemies speak evil against me:
>"When will she die and her name be obliterated?"
Even when my enemy comes to visit me,
>her concern is empty and false;
>her heart gathers malicious thoughts,
>>which she then goes out and spreads.
Together, they whisper against me, all my enemies,
>they plot evil against me, they explain my suffer-
>>ing away.
"All her evil has returned to haunt her through this illness,"
>they say,
>"And now that she has succumbed,
>she will never get up again."
Even my intimate friend,
>whom I trusted, who ate my bread,
>has turned on me, has ambushed me!

But You, Adonai,
> Take pity on me,
> Be gracious to me,
> Lift me up and I shall repay them.
By Your healing, I will know that You accept me,
> that my enemy does not shout triumphantly
>> over me.
You will support me because of my integrity,
> You will let me abide in Your presence forever.
Praised is Adonai, God of Israel,
> from eternity to eternity—
> Amen and Amen!

Psalm 42

To the Chief Musician; Instruction to the Sons of Korach

Like a hind crying for springs of water,
> so my soul cries out to You, O God.
My soul thirsts for God,
> for the living *El*/Almighty;
> O, when will I come to appear before God?
My tears have been my food,
> day and night;
> my enemies taunt me all day, asking,
> "Where is your God?"
This I remember, and pour out my soul within me—
> how I used to walk with the crowd,
> moving with them, the festive throng, up to the
House of God,
>> with joyous shouts of praise to God
>>> a multitude celebrating the festival!
Why so downcast, my soul?
> Why disquieted within me?
>> Have hope in God!
>>> For I will yet praise God
>>> for deliverance, for God's presence.
My God, my soul is cast down within me;
> as I remember You in the land of the Jordan River,
>> and Mount Hermon's peaks,
>>> and the smaller mountain of Sinai.
Deep cries out to deep,
> the sounds of the opened sluices of heaven;

all Your breakers and Your billows
    have swept over me.
By day, Adonai will command Divine loving abundance
  of kindness,
      and at night, God's resting place will be with me;
        This is my prayer to the Almighty, God of
        my life.
      I say to the Almighty, my Rock:
          "Why have You forgotten me?
          "Why must I walk in dark gloom,
             oppressed by enemies?"
Crushing my bones
    my adversaries revile me,
    taunting me all day with,
      "Where is your God?"
Why so downcast, my soul?
    Why disquieted within me?
    Have hope in God!
      I will yet praise God,
        My ever-present Help,
          my God.

Psalm 59

To the Chief Musician, a precious song of David:

    "Destroy not!"
Composed when Saul sent messengers to surround
      David's house and kill him.
Rescue me from enemies, my God;
    from those who rise up against me—strengthen
      me!
Rescue me from those who act treacherously;
from bloodthirsty people—save me!
For they lie in ambush for my soul,
    brazen ones gather against me;
    yet I have not transgressed,
      nor sinned against them, Adonai!
    With no wrongdoing on my part,
      they run and prepare themselves—
        Awake, come towards me and see!
    You, Adonai, God of Hosts,
    God of Israel,
      Rise up,

Hold all peoples accountable;
Show no favor to sinful traitors, *Selah*.
They return toward evening, howling
like dogs,
going round about the city;
Mouths barking,
Swords in their lips,
"Who hears it? Who cares?" they say.
But You, Adonai, You laugh at them,
You scorn the evil among the nations.
My strength—
for Your Help I wait,
for God is my Haven.
God, my Faithful One,
You will go before me;
God will let me gaze upon watchful foes.
Do not kill them, lest my people forget;
remove them from prosperity, with Your power,
and bring them down,
Our Shield, my Master.
For the sin of their mouth is the word of their lips,
their very pride will trap them,
because of the curses and lies that they tell.
Consume them in wrath;
Consume them that they exist no more:
and then they will know
That God rules in Jacob
to the ends of the earth, *Selah*.
The wicked may return toward evening,
howling like dogs,
going round about the city;
wandering about, searching for food,
they do not sleep until they are satiated.
But as for me
I will sing of Your strength
I will sing out loud in the morning,
rejoicing in Your loving abundance of
kindness;
For You have been my Stronghold,
a Refuge for me on my day of
trouble.
My Strength—

to You I will sing praises,
for God is my Tower of Strength,
God is my loving abundance of
kindness.

Psalm 77

To the Chief Musician:

On the sufferings of evil decrees; A song of Asaph.
I lift my voice to God and cry out;
I lift my voice to You
and You turn Your ears to hear.
On my day of suffering
I seek out my Master;
At night, my hand reaches out,
without ceasing;
My soul refuses to be comforted.
I remember God—and I moan;
When I talk,
my spirit faints, *Selah.*
You gripped the lids of my eyes;
I throbbed in pain, and could not speak.
I recall former days—
ancient years, time long past;
I remember my song, well into the night;
I delve into my heart,
My spirit searches and seeks.
Will my Master cast me off forever?
Will You not show favor to me once again?
Has Your loving abundance of kindness disap-
peared once and for all?
Has Your word come to an end—
for all generations?
Has the Almighty forgotten how to be gracious?
Has Your anger shut out Your mercy, *Selah?*
I said, "It is to terrify me, to inspire me with fear,
that the Right Hand of the Most High has shifted."
I remember the deeds of God,
I remember Your wonders from days long ago.
I meditate on all Your work, Your actions,
I speak of Your deeds.
God: Holiness is Your way—
What power is as great as God?

You are the Almighty who does wonders,
    You have let the nations know of Your strength.
You redeemed Your people with an outstretched arm,
    the children of Jacob and Joseph, *Selah*.
The waters saw you, God,
        the waters saw you and were terrified;
            The depths trembled in turmoil!
The clouds poured out water,
        the skies emitted thunderclaps,
            Your hailstone arrows flew about!
The sound of Your thunder
        whirled like a wheel,
            Bolts of lightning illumined the world,
                the earth trembled and quaked.
Your way was in the sea
        Your path was in the great waters
            Your footsteps were not visible.
You led Your people as a flock,
        by the hand of Moses and Aaron.

Psalm 90

A prayer of Moses, a man of God:

        Adonai, You have been a refuge for us
    in every generation.
Before the mountains were born,
        before You brought forth the earth and the
                            inhabited world.
            from world to world—
                You are the Almighty.
You bring people down
        from arrogance to contrition;
            You say,
                "Return to Me, children of Adam
                and Eve!"
For a thousand years are in Your eyes
        like yesterday, which has just passed,
            like a watch in the night.
The stream of human life is like a dream;
        In the morning, it is as grass, sprouting fresh;
        In the morning, it blossoms and flourishes;
            but by evening, it is cut down and shrivels.
So are we consumed by Your anger;

we are terrified by Your rage.
You have placed our sins before You;
    Our hidden misdeeds
        are exposed by the light of Your counte-
        nance.
All our days vanish
    in the glare of Your wrath;
    We have used up our years,
        which pass like a word unspoken.
The days of our years may total seventy;
    if we are exceptionally strong, perhaps eighty;
        but all their pride and glory is toil and
        falsehood,
            and, severed quickly, we fly away.
Who can know the force of Your fury?
    Your rage is as awful as our fear!
To count every day—teach us,
    so we will acquire a heart of wisdom.
Return, Adonai—how long?
    Take pity, have compassion on Your servants.
Satisfy us in the morning
    with Your loving abundance of kindness,
    and we will sing and rejoice all our days!
Give us joy
    that will challenge the days of our affliction,
        the years we have seen evil.
Let Your work be revealed to Your servants,
    let Your splendor be on their children.
May the pleasantness of my Master, our God, rest upon us,
    and may the work of our hands be established;
        Establish the work of our hands!

Psalm 105

Give thanks to Adonai, call upon God's name;

    Let all nations know about God's deeds!
Sing to God, compose songs, play instruments for God;
    Tell all about God's wondrous acts!
Take pride in God's Holy reputation;
    The heart of those who seek God rejoices!
Search for Adonai and for God's might,
    Seek God's presence always!
Remember the wonders God has performed,

God's miracles, and the laws from God's mouth.
Seed of Abraham, God's servant,
    Children of Jacob, God's chosen:
You are Adonai, our God;
    The whole earth is governed by Your laws.
You remembered Your eternal covenant,
    the word which You commanded to a thousand
      generations.
The covenant which You made with Abraham,
    Your oath to Isaac—
You established it as a statute for Jacob,
    for Israel—an everlasting covenant.
Saying,
    "To you I will give the land of Canaan,
      the portion of your inheritance."
When they were only few in number,
    and had scarcely dwelled in the land;
when they wandered from nation to nation,
    from one kingdom to another people—
You permitted no one to oppress them;
    You admonished kings on their behalf:
      "Do not touch My anointed ones,
        and to My prophets do no harm."
You called a famine in the land,
    their staff of life, their bread, You broke off.
Before them, You sent a man—
    Joseph, sold as a slave.
They weighed his legs down in fetters,
    an iron chain on his soul.
Until Your word came to pass,
    the word of Adonai purified him.
The king sent messengers and released him,
    the ruler of many peoples set him free.
He appointed him master over his house,
    ruler over his possessions,
      binding his ministers to his soul,
      making his elders wise.
Israel then came down to Egypt
    Jacob sojourned in the land of Ham.
God made God's people extremely fruitful,
    You made them stronger than their adversaries,
      whose hearts You turned to hate Your
      people,

        to conspire against Your servants.
You sent Moses, Your servant,
     and Aaron, whom You had chosen.
They performed among them
     words of Your signs,
         wonders in the land of Ham.
You sent darkness—and it was dark;
     they did not rebel against Your word.
You turned their waters into blood,
     causing their fish to die.
Their land swarmed with frogs,
     reaching the very chambers of the kings.
You spoke, and wild beasts came,
     lice throughout their borders.
You turned their rains into hail,
     flaming fire in their land.
     The hail struck their vines and fig trees,
         shattered the trees within their borders.
God spoke and locusts came,
     beetles beyond number.
     They ate every herb in their land,
         they devoured the fruit of their soil.
You struck all the firstborn in their land,
     the prime of their strength.
You brought them out, carrying silver and gold,
     and none among Your tribes stumbled.
Egypt rejoiced when they departed,
     for their terror had fallen upon them.
You spread out a cloud as a sheltering cover,
     a fire to illumine the night.
Israel asked and You provided quail,
     You satisfied them with bread from Heaven.
You broke open a rock and waters gushed out,
     rushing through dry places like a river.
For You remembered Your holy word, Your promise
     to Abraham, Your servant.
You brought out Your people with gladness,
     Your chosen ones with joyful singing.
You gave them the lands of nations,
     they inherited that which nations acquire by labor.
So that they might keep Your statutes,
     and treasure Your teachings,
        Halleluyah!

Psalm 137

By the rivers of Babylon,
    there we sat and we wept
        as we remembered Zion.
Upon the willows on its banks
    we hung up our harps.
For there our captors demanded of us
    words of song;
        Our tormentors asked of us (with) joy:
            "Sing to us from the songs of Zion!"
But how shall we sing the song of Adonai
    on alien soil?
If I ever forget you, Jerusalem,
    may my right hand forget its cunning!
May my tongue cleave to the roof of my mouth,
    if I remember you not;
        if I do not set Jerusalem
            above my highest joy!
Remind the sons of Edom, Adonai, about the day of
Jerusalem—
    remind those who said,
        "Raze it, raze it to its very foundation!"
Daughter of Babylon,
    it is you who are the annihilated one;
        Happy is the one who will repay you
            For all that you have done to us!
Happy is the one who will grab your little ones,
    dashing them against the rock!

Psalm 150

Halleluyah. Praise God!
    Praise God in God's Sanctuary;
    Praise God
        in the vast expense of Heaven!
Praise God for mighty deeds;
    Praise God
        according to God's abundant greatness!
Praise God
    with the blowing of the *shofar;*
        Praise God
            with the lyre and the harp!
Praise God

with drum and dance;
>Praise God
>>with instruments and flute!
Praise God
>with resounding cymbals!
>>Praise God
>>>with clanging cymbals!
Let every breath of life praise God,
>*Halleluyah.* Praise God!

Things to remember:

Rabbi Nachman of Bratzlav was a Hasidic master who lived from 1772–1810. He identified ten psalms that he believed to contain the power to bring a complete healing to body and spirit. He called these psalms a *tikkun klali*, a complete healing. Nachman was the great-grandson of the Baal Shem Tov, the founder of Hasidism. Although he was joyful, there was a pessimistic streak in him which is epitomized in his often-quoted teaching (frequently put to music), "The world is a narrow bridge. The important thing is not to be afraid." When Rabbi Nachman died, his followers did not select a successor to him.

Key words and phrases:

Tehillim: psalms
Tikkun klali: complete healing or complete remedy

If you want to know more:

Simkha Y. Weintraub, ed., *Healing of Soul, Healing of Body: Spiritual Leaders Unfold the Strength and Solace in Psalms.* Woodstock, VT: Jewish Lights Publishing, 1994.

Index to Volumes I-III